Where They Lived

Historic Clare Michigan Homes
and the
People Who Lived in Them

Kenneth Lingaur

Lingaur Preservation LLC
Clare, Michigan
2017

Lingaur Preservation L.L.C.
Clare, Michigan
www.lingaurpreservation.com
Printed in the U.S.A.

ISBN-13: 978-0-692-98560-1
ISBN-10: 0-692-98560-3

To Sherrie,

no man could ask for a better wife.

Table of Contents

Table of Contents
With Clare Homes in
Alphabetical Order

Acknowledgements

First and foremost, I would like to thank my wife, Sherrie. She has encouraged me along the way in this project, despite my feeling that she would prefer me to work on the honey-do list around the house. Without her, this book would not be.

I would also like to thank Robert Knapp. Robert was a source of encouragement through the writing of this book, and a help with historic information. In addition, he provided me with photographs not found in the Forrest Meek collection. Robert was also instrumental in funding the digitizing of the Clare historic newspapers by the Clarke Historical Library at Central Michigan University. This book would not be as complete, and not have been able to be produced as quickly as it was without the ability to search the newspapers in a digital manner online. He has become the first person I go to for anything related to Clare history.

No book written about the history of Clare would be possible without the prior research done by Forrest Meek. Meek was the best historian Clare has had, and was responsible for the rebirth of interest in Clare's history. I am particularly thankful to Forrest Meek for his collection of historic photographs.

Other people assisting in this book have been my niece, Shelbie Groot, who read through the book and gave editing suggestions, and Heather Todd, who designed the cover and the maps located in the book.

Thanks are also given to the staff at both the Clare County Register of Deeds Office and the Clare County Treasurer's Office. They were always very friendly and helpful during my weekly visits.

I would also like to thank the people that read this book. Your interest in the history of Clare is why people like me do what we do.

Thank You

Introduction

I love to research historic architecture. I enjoy learning about who owned buildings, who lived in houses, when they were built, and in some cases finding out when they were lost. My training and work are primarily as an architectural historian.

A lot of what I do deals with actual architecture. However, to many people, architecture can be boring. The focus of this book is to discuss the people who lived in the houses of Clare, Michigan. It is not my plan to give a complete chronology of every owner of the houses listed in this book. Only the owners from the time of construction of the house until about the mid-twentieth century are featured here. Information is plentiful on some people, and lacking on others. If I didn't write about one person as much as I do another, it might be more from a lack of information than a lack of interest.

The houses in this book are organized by their date of construction. The oldest houses are listed first followed by the newer ones in chronological order. Both sections of the book, Historic Homes and Lost but not Forgotten Homes, are organized separately in this manner.

To obtain the information for this book a considerable amount of time was spent researching deeds at the Clare County Register of Deeds Office. That information gave me the history of who owned each house and when they owned them. From there I located those names in the historic Clare newspapers and learned about the people through the articles written about them. Sometimes the newspapers would cover when people were building houses. For the houses where that information could not be found, I researched tax records at the Clare County Treasurer's Office.

For each house featured in this book I have tried to provide the year of construction, a chronology of ownership, and a brief history of each owner.

My hope is that after you read this book you will look at the houses featured here and not look at them as just old houses. I hope you will see them as places where people that were important to the history of Clare used to live. They are places that are uniquely Clare, and they have value to the community.

When I started this book my hope was to feature about one hundred houses. I tried to find every house in Clare that was constructed with brick, had a stone foundation, and/or just looked old.

When I started the research I realized I needed to reduce that number. I had about a one year time frame to finish the book, and saw that with the time it took to research just one house, I would not meet my deadline. The houses that were finally included were ones that I thought were interesting to the majority of Clarites, and several more that were interesting to me.

I relied on the Forrest Meek collection at Mid Michigan Community College and Robert Knapp for historic photographs in the book, but I also included photographs from the historic newspapers. I believed a bad picture was better than no picture, so forgive me for including the low quality newspaper photographs in the book.

I hope you enjoy reading about the historic homes of Clare as much as I enjoyed researching and writing about them.

CLARE - West of McEwan

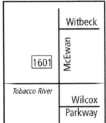

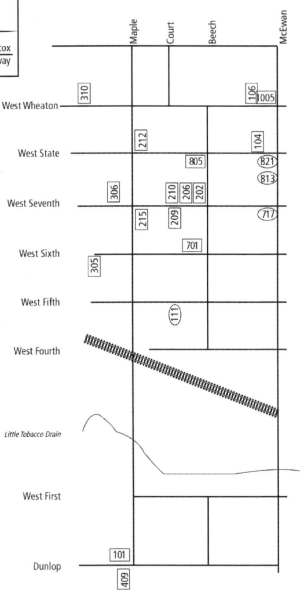

CLARE - East of McEwan

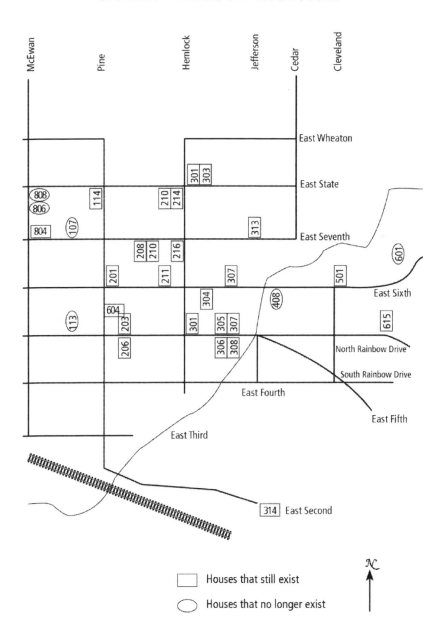

Houses that still exist

Houses that no longer exist

𝒩

Part I

Historic

Homes

702 Center Avenue, Bay City, Michigan
Constructed in 1859

How does a common machinist from Scotland come to the United States, make himself one of the important developers of a major Michigan city, and go on to found a small town in the center of the state? The houses in this book are located in Clare, that small town in the center of the state. And although not a house found in Clare this house, which was owned by William McEwan, is no less important to the history of Clare.

William McEwan was born on either March 5, 1823, or March 10, 1824, depending on which biography you read. He was the youngest of seven children born to William Sr. & Margaret McEwan. The place of his birth was Glasgow, Scotland, where he lived until he came with his family to the United States in 1848. They first arrived in New York City where they lived for a few months, then on to Detroit for two years, and finally to Chicago.

10

William was trained as a pattern maker and machinist while in Scotland, working in the Napier Steamship building plant in Glasgow. He continued with that profession after coming to America. In his spare time he and his brother Alexander built sawmill machinery, and in the autumn of 1850 brought the machinery to what was then called Lower Saginaw (Bay City). When arriving there they purchased a mill site from James Fraser, one of the founders of Bay City, and the eventual father-in-law of William McEwan. Their brother John joined the partnership with the two brothers in 1851.

While continuing his partnership with his brothers, William McEwan also built Bay City's first grist mill in 1857 which lasted several years, formed a mill partnership with John J. Fraser in 1865 which lasted for about one year, and promoted and superintended the construction of Bay City's street railway system.

He married Annie Fraser in 1858 and built this house on Center Avenue (although drastically remodeled since the time of its original construction) in 1859 (see photograph below). The land McEwan

William and Annie McEwan's Residence
From the late nineteenth century
Photograph from the Collection of the
Bay County Historical Society

chose for his house was considered "desolate enough, being covered with stumps, through which wound a tortuous path to the forest just beyond." Little did he know Center Avenue would become one of the most desired locations in Bay City to construct a house. Many fine houses were built on this avenue during Bay City's history. In fact many of these homes have been listed on the National Register of Historic Places, as part of the Center Avenue Neighborhood Residential District since 2012.

In the mid-1860s McEwan began purchasing land in Clare County for the purpose of cutting timber and transporting it downriver to his sawmill in Bay City. The area where the City of Clare is now located was not cleared of lumber until about 1868. It was about this time of McEwan's life that he began stepping away from active business, and started his life of retirement. William's brother John continued the McEwan sawmill business until his death in 1882. His brother Alexander had passed away many years before in either 1854 or 1855.

The remainder of William McEwan's life was devoted to his real estate interests. It was in 1870 that the town of Clare was platted, and McEwan would spend the rest of his life selling off lots in the village. In addition to the lots he owned within the village of Clare, McEwan was also selling cutover land to farmers, along with property within Bay City.

The last fourteen years of McEwan's life saw his health decline. It is not known when, but at some time in his life, he suffered from partial deafness. This was most likely caused from his early days of working in machine shops. His ill health prompted him to find relief twice on trips to his native Scotland, and he also spent several winters in California. William McEwan passed away on one of those trips to California on March 10, 1887. One surprising fact about McEwan was that although he had been in America for almost forty years, he never became a naturalized citizen.

Annie McEwan continued with her husband's real estate interests after his death. McEwan's First Addition to the Village of Clare was approved four months after the death of William McEwan. The plat map bears the name of both Annie and William's son, William, as executors of the "last will and testament of William McEwan deceased Proprietor."

Annie McEwan lived in the house at 702 Center Avenue, Bay City until 1913 when she moved to Seattle, Washington to live with her son Alexander. Her son Allan owned the house after Annie moved. Allan was born in this house in 1865 and died here in 1935. Allan's wife Jennie lived in the house until the late 1930s. The house was sold to the Bay City Public School in the early 1940s. By the early 1950s, it had been converted to an apartment building and has continued to serve that function to this day.

409 Dunlop Street
Constructed in 1876

This house was constructed by Ephraim Taylor in 1876. No information could be found on Ephraim Taylor other than he lived in Vernon Township prior to buying this property. He owned the house for two years before selling to Nathan and Martha Bicknell in December 1877.

Nathan Bicknell was born in 1847, the son of a doctor from Camden East, Ontario. Before moving to Clare he was working for a large mercantile business in Napanee, Ontario. He married Martha Henry in 1867. Martha was a native of Napanee and was born in 1850. The Bicknell family came to Clare in 1874. Nathan first worked as a teacher in the Grout Township School in Gladwin County. He also supplemented his income as an auctioneer. After teaching he worked as the manager of the Nichols Hotel in Clare. In the late 1870s he purchased a store building in the south part of

Nathan and Martha Bicknell
Nathan Bicknell photograph from the Forrest Meek Collection
Martha Bicknell photograph from the Clare Courier 1903

town, and there he started his mercantile business. George Halstead bought out Bicknell's grocery stock in 1881, and Nathan focused his store business on dry goods. In 1898 he constructed a brick store building on the east side of the 400 Block of North McEwan. He built his Bicknell Department Store building in 1907 north of and adjacent to his existing brick store.

Nathan passed away in 1909 from heart problems. Martha survived him and lived in this house until her death in 1918. Melvin and Elsie Brasington purchased the house ten months after Martha's passing.

Melvin was born in Oakland County near Pontiac in 1868. When he was twelve years old his family moved to a farm in Gilmore Township. Melvin would later marry Elsie Owens, and they lived on the Brasington family farm. At the time Melvin and Elsie purchased the home at 409 Dunlop Street Melvin was fifty-one years old.

The Brasingtons sold the house to Charles and Lillian Stirling in 1928. Charles originated from Union Township in Isabella County and was born in 1876. He attended the Ontario Veterinary College in Toronto, Canada and graduated in 1904. He first set up a veterinary office in Remus but relocated to Clare in 1905. In Clare, his office was located in the Thayer feed barn.

He married Lillian Ludy of Shepherd in 1906. She was born in 1877 in Isabella County. Dr. Stirling lived in this house until he passed away in 1963. Lillian preceded him in death one year earlier. After Charles' death, the house was deeded to his son Dr. Neil Stirling who was also a veterinarian.

Nathan Bicknell Residence and Farm
Drawing from the 1884 Clare, Michigan Birds-Eye View
Looking northwest
O. H. Bailey & Co. Publishers Boston
From the Robert Knapp Collection

301 East Fifth Street
Constructed in 1883

When looking back at our family trees it is everyone's hope that they are descendants of royalty. Clark H. Sutherland, a descendant of the Scottish Duke of Sutherland, could actually claim he was. It is unknown when his family emigrated from Scotland to America, and under what circumstances, but Clark was born in Deerfield Michigan in 1851. Along with his parents, he came to Clare in 1873. He started his employment in a saw mill, but soon started his own blacksmith shop and later sold fruit trees. He married Rose Alger in 1877.

Rose was born in 1860 in Cramby, Ontario, Canada to Peter and Isabella Alger. The Alger's came to the Clare area in 1866 and eventually opened one of Clare's first hotels, the Alger House, sometime between 1870 and 1871.

Clark and Rose Sutherland
Photographs from the Forrest Meek Collection

While the county seat was located in Farwell, Mr. Sutherland was elected the Clare County Register of Deeds. Two years later, in 1878, he was reelected as the Register of Deeds and also elected as the County Clerk. In 1880 he was reelected to both offices, this time serving in Harrison which was awarded the county seat in 1879. When his time of service to the county was ended he returned to Clare and built this house in 1883. Upon returning to Clare he began work in the hardware business. His hardware days lasted for a short time. In 1885 Clark Sutherland along with William Wolskey, C. W. Perry, and Louis Weisman started the Clare County Bank. The bank was originally located in a small building on the northwest corner of the lot where 524 North McEwan is now located. In 1887 they moved to Alfred Doherty's new brick building on the southeast corner of Fifth and McEwan Streets. It would move again in 1922 when the bank constructed its own building on the northwest corner of Fourth and McEwan Streets. Clark was the bank's cashier from the time it opened until it closed in 1932.

Clark passed away in 1943 at the age of ninety-one. His health was so poor the last five years of his life that he was bedridden. After Clark's death, the house was deeded to Sutherland's daughter and son-in-law, Avis and Homer Douglas. Rose continued to live in this house under the care of her daughter until she passed away at the age of eighty-eight in 1948. Clark and Rose lived in the house sixty years and sixty-five years respectively.

The year after Rose's death, the Douglas' sold the house to Harold and Vivian Hughes.

Harold was a native of Ithaca, being born there in 1911. His family moved to Harrison and he graduated high school there in 1929. He graduated from the Central State Teachers College in 1933. He then taught for two years in the Harrison School system. He went back to college and graduated from the Detroit College of Law in 1939. Harold married Vivian Baughman, in Shepherd, in 1938.

While Harold was in Detroit he was a professor at the Detroit Institute of

Harold Hughes
Photograph from the
Clare Sentinel 1945

Technology. He later resigned to become an attorney for the Industrial Bank of Detroit. He came to Clare in 1945 to start his own law office in the Citizens State Bank building on the northeast corner of Fourth and McEwan Streets. While in Clare he went on to become the Clare County Prosecuting Attorney from 1946 to 1954. He would also serve as the attorney for the City of Clare. He served as a State Senator from 1963 to 1967. The Hughes continued to live in the house until the mid-1960s.

301 East Fifth Street
Unknown Date
Photograph from the Forrest Meek Collection

201 East Sixth Street
Constructed in 1883

At the time of his death in 1937, Jacob Mason was one of three surviving veterans of the Civil War still residing in Clare.

He fought with Company E of the 29th Regiment. He came to Clare in 1872 and was engaged in the lumber business. He married Martha Eaton in 1875.

Martha was a native of Goodrich, Michigan, being born in 1846, and arrived in Clare the year before Jacob. In 1883 the *Clare County Press* noted that Jacob was the local agent for the Morton & Barney cement company out of Flint.

Later Jacob formed a partnership with James S. Boyd and opened a grocery store in the Wolskey Block. The earliest mention of this business in the Clare newspaper is in February 1890. Besides being in the grocery business Jacob was the second mayor of Clare, served as an alderman and supervisor, and Under Sherriff for Clare County.

Jacob Mason built this house in 1883 and lived here until 1897. He traded this house with William Becker, for Becker's farm in Sheridan Township.

William Becker was born in Wallaceburg, Ontario, in 1862. He moved with his family to the Clare area in 1881. He married Nettie Gordon in 1891, and she passed away eight years later.

Nettie was born in 1856 in Ayre, Ontario. She moved with her parents to Lapeer County when she was still very young. She also came to the Clare area in 1881 and was a school teacher in the Bradley, Eagle, and Hatton Schools.

When William and Nettie came to Clare in 1897, William opened a saloon business with George Dawson in Dawson's building. On January 1, 1898, Dawson bought out William's interest in the business. Two months later Becker formed a partnership with Elmer Halstead in a grocery business located in George Dawson's brick block at 427 North McEwan.

Dr. Allen Mulder purchased this house from the Beckers in 1899.

Dr. Mulder came to Clare in 1894, and took over the dental practice of Dr. C. H. Edwards, locating his office in the Dunlop Building. Mulder was a recent graduate of the University of Michigan Dental School. Allan Mulder was born in Laingsburg, Michigan in 1869. He married Lillian Crane in 1893.

Lillian was born in Dexter, Michigan, in 1869. Until she was eight years old she

Dr. Allen Mulder Family
Photograph from the
Forrest Meek Collection

22

had lived on a farm in Dexter Township, moving then to Victor, Clinton County.

When Allen Mulder sold this house in 1907 he still had an extensive future ahead of him in Clare. In 1908 he was elected vice president and chairman of the board for the newly organized Citizens State Bank. He held these positions until 1950 and served on the bank's board of directors until his death in 1951. He also served forty-three years on the Clare Board of Education. Thirty-two years of his service were spent as the board's president. He continued to practice dentistry until the age of seventy-nine, retiring in 1949.

Between 1907 and 1912 the house changed hands three times. In this time period it was first owned by Colin McDonald, then William Bowler, and finally Joseph Bowler. It is unknown how long Colin McDonald lived here, and it is not certain if William or Joseph Bowler ever lived here. Joseph was advertising this house as available for rent in 1916. In fact, it appears that this was a rental property from then until about 1979.

Joseph Bowler sold this property to Bertelle Waite in 1918. The Clare County Savings Bank took it over from Bertelle Waite in 1932. One year later the house was purchased by Alfred and Delphernia Loomis. The Loomises owned the house until 1953 when they sold it to Marjorie Walworth. The house would then stay in the Walworth family until 1979.

The known people who have rented here are: Mrs. J. H. Wilson early to mid-1920s, Mrs. Fred Border early 1930s, Mrs. Lottie Dawson mid-1930s, Bus Comer late 1930s, and Edward Jr. and Donna Bailey from the early 1940s to late 1970s.

Edward Bailey Jr. was born in 1913, and Donna Smalley was born in 1914. They were married in 1933 in Kalamazoo. It is unknown when they came to Clare, but they were living in this house in 1942 when Edward enlisted in the Navy and fought in World War II. Donna had been employed at Holly Carburetor, was a waitress at the Doherty Hotel, and was an office clerk at Clare City Hall.

306 East Fifth Street
Constructed in 1883

This house was constructed in 1883 by George Raven. Little is known about Mr. Raven. He is first mentioned in Clare newspapers in 1880. In 1884 he is mentioned as being in partnership with Calvin B. Keyes in a building located on the east side of the 100 block of North McEwan Street. There are no other references of him in the newspaper after 1884, but his wife is noted as living on Sixth Street in 1886.

Josiah Horning purchased this house in 1885 and owned it until the fall of 1889. The January 30, 1880, edition of the *Clare County Press* first reports on Josiah Horning as putting in shingle mill machinery in the Ort planning mill. He also ran a shingle mill in Loomis in 1883. Although he was insured, a fire at his Clare shingle mill in May 1889 was a considerable loss to him. He ended up selling his business and this house later that year to find a better business location for his shingle mill. He returned to Clare the following year.

Charles and Katherine Ackerman bought this house from Horning in 1889. Charles was born in 1832 and was a native of Tonawanda, New York. He married the twenty-two-year-old Katherine Durban in 1854. She was born in Baden Germany and came to America in 1852. They came to Northern Isabella County in 1886 and three years later purchased this house in Clare. Their time at this house on Fifth was short. They sold it in 1902 and moved to Herman Lange's house on State Street.

Joseph and Rachel Hudson purchased the house from the Ackermans. Joseph had an interesting life before coming to Clare. He was born in Yorkshire England in 1850. When he was thirteen years of age he started working as a shipbuilder. He later obtained a job on a sailing vessel and worked on the ship that carried the expedition in search of David Livingston to Africa. Another one of his voyages is retold from his obituary:

> He was shipwrecked and with others spent several days on the high seas in an open boat. Their food and water were exhausted and their strength was well-nigh spent, when they were discovered and taken aboard a sailing vessel bound for Buenos Ayres. The discovery of the little boat was brought about by a lad, who with his mother was a passenger on the ship, and was on the ship's bridge with the first mate. The mate had given the lad permission to look through the glass and he saw the boat with its load of perishing men. The boy succeeded in getting the attention of the ship's officer and the vessel hove-to and took the men on board.

Joseph Hudson worked on the sailing ships for about five years. After this, he immigrated to Quebec, Canada, and then came to the Detroit area. When he arrived in the United States he obtained work in the brickyard near the town of Fordson. In 1868 he came to

Clare County and spent the winter in the lumber camp near the present site of the City of Clare. After the river drive in the spring, he relocated to Ionia where he met and married his wife Rachel Cross in 1870. They moved to Grant Township in November 1870 and purchased 40 acres in the middle of Section Two. Except for a short period where they lived in Missouri, they spent thirty-two years on the farm before moving into this house.

Joseph Hudson
Photograph from the
Forrest Meek Collection

In addition to his farming interests, Mr. Hudson was one of the original incorporators of the Clare County Savings Bank when it became a state bank in 1891. He was the first treasurer for the Board of Control for the Michigan School for the Blind in Saginaw when it was built and later served as the organization's president. His obituary also credits him as being responsible for clearing much of the timber north of Clare.

Joseph Hudson passed away while living in this house in 1929. His wife Rachel followed him in death fourteen months later. After their deaths, the house was deeded to the Hudson's granddaughters Leah and Rachel. They were the daughters of Joseph and Rachel's son Fred, who at the time lived at the house immediately to the east (308 East Fifth). Rachel was married to Carl Garchow, and Leah was married to Carl's brother William Garchow Jr. Carl and Rachel lived in Pontiac starting in 1926, so they could not have lived in this house.

William and Leah lived in the house until at least 1941. William was born in 1898 while his family was farming in Grant

Township. When he was nine years old his family moved to the Colonville area in Sheridan Township. He married Leah Hudson in 1921.

Leah was born in 1897 when her parents owned a farm in Grant Township. Leah graduated from Clare High School in 1915. She went on to finish her education at the Mount Pleasant Normal School and taught in the rural Clare schools for the following seven and a half years.

William and Leah moved to Clare in 1924. William worked as a substitute mail carrier for the next twenty-five years. In addition, he worked as an "interior-exterior decorator and painter." Many Clare homes were improved as a result of his work.

In 1942 William and Leah moved to 502 East Sixth Street. Rachel and Carl Garchow's interest in the house was transferred to William and Leah after Rachel's death in 1955. Leah retained ownership of the house until 1967.

202 West Seventh Street
Constructed in 1884

If the term lumber baron were applied to anyone, it would definitely be used to describe Ammi Wright. Ammi Wright was a major lumberman from Saginaw, Michigan in the mid-nineteenth century. Wright, along with William McEwan, were the two main lumbermen in the Clare area in the early 1860s. What is now present day McEwan Street in Clare represents what was then the property line between McEwan's and Wright's properties, McEwan owned the property to the west of McEwan Street, and Wright owned to the east. In September 1864 McEwan purchased Wright's tract of land, making him the owner of all the land making up the future village of Clare.

In 1860, Edward Pratt, an eighteen-year-old man from Elgin County, Ontario, Canada, emigrated to Saginaw and started his employment with the Wright & Company business. He started working in their saw mill and later became a foreman in the mill. He eventually moved to Clare County and managed the farm that Wright owned. The farm was cultivated using the cut-over land that Wright owned and was used to grow everything needed to feed his lumber camps which operated in the winters.

Pratt married the nineteen-year-old Melissa Trombley in 1868. Melissa was originally from Montreal, Canada. Six years later Edward purchased his own large tract of land in Clare County.

Pratt ran a number of camps each winter cutting timber

Edward Pratt
Photograph from the
Forrest Meek Collection

in Clare County from about 1874 until 1889. Edward Pratt formed partnerships with a number of men during his business days. Although it is unknown when it started, a partnership with J. E. Lexley was dissolved in 1884. Another partnership with Thomas Presley was dissolved in 1886.

Pratt's lumbering headquarters was located in the Village of Clare, and to say that Clare benefitted from Pratt & Company is an understatement. During the 1888 to 1889 lumber season, Pratt & Company paid out an estimated $75,000.00 to his employees in the Village of Clare.

Although Edward Pratt owned a farm with a house about three miles north of Clare, he built this house on Seventh Street in 1884. He most likely stayed here when in town for business, and lived in the farm house north of Clare at other times. As the lumbering era of Clare County came to an end (the winter of 1888-1889 was the last Pratt lumbering season reported by Clare newspapers), Edward Pratt found other means of business to occupy his time. In the summer of 1889, Pratt went into partnership with Jake Kennedy starting a livery in a barn on Fourth Street.

Edward and Melissa Pratt owned this house until 1890 when they sold it to Rollin H. Jenney. For most of the time Rollin owned this house he called it his residence. His family lived here, but his place of employment was out of town. The Union Iron Co. with locations in Gaston and Yuma, Michigan, where he served as superintendent, was one of those out of town jobs. Mr. Rollin did have some employment in Clare. Starting in 1892 and ending the next year, Rollin was the general manager of the Clare Wooden Ware Company. In addition, he was named to the Board of Directors of the Clare County State Bank in 1895.

In 1899 Rollin Jenney changed jobs and accepted the superintendent position for the Antrim Iron Company in Mancelona, Michigan. This time his family moved with him and he sold the house two years later to Dr. Fred C. and Mary Sanford.

Dr. Sanford was born in 1864 in Liberty Township, Jackson County, Michigan. When he was three years old his family moved to Otisville in Genesee County, then later to Flint, and finally in 1870 to Lincoln Township, Isabella County. Until he was fourteen he attended the district school, for two years attended Mount Pleasant High School, and then another two years at Hillsdale College. After teaching in the rural schools for five and a half years, Sanford attended the Homeopathic Department of the University of Michigan and

Dr. Fred C. Sanford
Photograph from the
Clare Sentinel 1952

30

graduated in 1890. That same year he came to Clare and practiced medicine here until his death in 1952.

Dr. Sanford was married first in 1886 to Mary Gunnel, who was born in Mount Pleasant in 1867. Fred and Mary had one son, Dr. B. J. Sanford, who survived two years of service in World War

Lt. Glen Sanford
Photograph from the
Clare Sentinel 1943

I, and return to Clare to practice medicine in the community for many years.

Mary died in 1917, and the following year Dr. Sanford married Pearl Peters. Pearl was born in 1887 to Charles and Agnus Johnson of Clare. She married Nelson Peters in 1907, but he passed away the following year. Fred and Pearl had a son and daughter. Their son, Lt. Glen Sanford, was killed in 1943 when his plane came up missing while on maneuvers in Suisun Bay, California, during World War II. Pearl lived in this house until her death in 1954. Her daughter Lola Blystone inherited the house and owned it until 1970.

306 West Seventh Street
Constructed from 1885 to 1890

Of all the houses in this book, the early history of this house, until about 1928, is the most puzzling. The deed records for this house did not match up with the tax records, and the number of newspaper articles to clarify matters are sparse. So, using what information is available, the following narrative is the history of 306 West Seventh Street with possible errors.

According to the deeds, Charles W. Perry was the first person to purchase this lot from the McEwan Land Company in 1906. Since Perry lived in a house on the 100 block of West Fifth Street, he never lived here. The newspaper articles found for this property agree more with the tax records than with the deeds. As a result, until we reach 1928 the tax records will be used as the source of who lived here.

William Chard began construction of this house in 1885 and was not completed until 1890. The August 25, 1893, issue of the *Clare Sentinel* reports that "Wm. Chard has traded his city property to Will Huble for a span of bay horses." This does seem to be the correct time Chard sold the house but there is no other information linking Will Huble to this property. The tax records note the taxes being paid by a Charles Milinger from 1895 to 1904. There is no mention in the Clare newspapers of anyone with the last name of Milinger. It was most likely the tax records should have said Charles Niemeyer.

Charles Niemeyer originated from Sauquot, Oneida County, New York, and was born in 1852. He later moved with his parents to Clinton County and arrived in Clare in 1871. He was first employed in the woods and saw mills of Hinkleville. In 1879 he began his employment with the Pere Marquette Railroad. In 1881 he was promoted to construction foreman, which he worked at for the next sixteen years. He married Clara Iva Bellinger in 1878.

Clara was born in 1859 and was from Burton, Michigan. She came to Clare the same year as Charles and settled with her family on a farm in Grant Township.

Clara and Charles Niemeyer
Photograph from the Clare Sentinel 1928

The Niemeyers sold their house to George and Bernice Wells in 1904. George Wells came to Clare from Ithaca when he

33

purchased this house. It is unknown what type of work brought Mr. Wells to Clare. However, in 1910 he was named the district manager of the Northern Assurance Company, and later the same year he was the local manager for the Union Telephone Company.

According again to the tax records, the property changed hands four times between 1917 and 1928. These owners included Clarence and Mamie Boom, Mr. and Mrs. R. B. Comer, Glen and Grace Blystone, and finally Hannah Smalley.

Hannah Smalley was from Tuscarawas County, Ohio, being born there in 1846. When she was still a girl her family relocated to Noble County, Indiana. She married David Smalley of Indiana in 1867. They came to Michigan shortly after their marriage and settled near Colonville where she lived for the next sixty years. Her husband, who served as the first supervisor of Sheridan Township, passed away in 1911. Hannah moved to Clare when she purchased this house in 1928. Hannah died in this house in 1931 and her granddaughter, Ruth Larson, along with Ruth's husband Joseph inherited the house.

Joseph Larson was born in 1897, in the town of Williamsport, Pennsylvania. In 1900 he came with his parents and settled on a farm in Sheridan Township. He enlisted in the Navy in 1918 and served in World War I. While in the service he contracted tuberculosis, and never fully recovered. He married Ruth Davis, granddaughter of Hannah Smalley, also from Sheridan Township, in 1927. The Larsons sold this house in December 1936 and moved to a farm in Grant Township. In the spring of the following year, Joseph Larson had the following story written about him in the April 9, 1937, issue of the *Clare Sentinel*:

> This community was horrified when the story of this grimful shooting Wednesday evening taking the life of Fred Schug, of this city became known among the families and friends. Joseph Larson, of Grant Township, is held in custody of county officers charged with murder.
>
> As near as our representative can learn the gruesome crime took place at the Schug farm in

Grant Township 1½ miles north and ½ west of Clare which is located opposite of the Larson home, about 5:45 Wednesday night when Mr. Schug went to his farm to care for the chores. Reports are that Larson had quarreled with his wife at their home and left the house with a shot gun with the threat that "He would get Schug too," Mrs. Larson ran ahead in an effort to warn the neighbor but could not accomplish her aim. Schug was at the well house near the barn a distance of about 35 feet when sighted by his assailant, who immediately opened fire. The shot grazed his right arm and lodged in his back below the shoulder blades penetrating his lungs. Schug ran up the lane to the road before he collapsed and fell.

Neighbors hearing the shot arrived to give assistance but the body was lifeless…

Fred Schug age 45, resided on East State Street and drove to and from his farm each day. He leaves his widow, and two daughters, Ruth Marie and Barbara Lou, also an aged mother, Mrs. Caroline Schug, together with many relatives.

The murder of Fred Schug resulted in Joseph Larson being sentenced two to fifteen years in Jackson Prison. He ended up dying two years later at the Veterans Administration Hospital in Milwaukee, Wisconsin of unknown causes.

Herbert and Lovangie Randall purchased this house from the Larsons. Herbert was born in Saginaw in 1889 and came to Clare with his family at the age of seven. He married Lovangie Hubel in 1911.

Lovangie was born in 1890 to long-time Clare County residents Frederick and Phoebe Hubel. Herbert served as mayor of Clare in the mid-1940s but was more known as a carpenter and contractor. Herbert served as contractor for the Bullock School south of Midland in 1932 and was one of the construction supervisors for Clare City Hall in 1934. One smaller job he is famous for is the design and construction of the veterans honor roll monument in Clare City Park. Herbert and Lovangie moved outside of Clare City limits in 1948. They did not sell this house until 1954.

Floyd and Beatrice Rosier were the purchasers of this house from the Randalls. Floyd was from Woodstock, Illinois and was born there in 1893. He lived in Flint from 1925 to 1945. He married Beatrice Garner in 1937 while he was living in Flint. The year after coming to Clare Floyd purchased and operated the Twin Elms Country Club, four and a half miles north of Clare. In 1949 they purchased the Vogue Shop, a women's apparel store at 517 North McEwan Street. They owned the Vogue Shop until 1953. Floyd was also a salesman at the Art Damoth real estate office in the early 1950s.

The Rosiers owned the house until 1957 when they sold to Jay and Maxine Green. The Rosiers moved to Mount Morris, in May 1957, after selling the house. Floyd passed away one month later.

206 East Fifth Street
Constructed in 1885

David Rorison was born in 1862, in Carleton Place, Ontario. His grandparents and mother originated from Paisley, Scotland. David came to Clare in 1880 where he made a career of selling hardware. He married his wife Marie in 1883, whom he met after moving to Clare. She was born in Amersberg, Canada, in 1862.

It is unknown where Rorison first worked when he arrived in Clare, but when A. J. Doherty started his hardware business in 1885, Rorison was one of his first employees. The following year he left the Doherty hardware store to succeed John Webb as the manager of Trevidick's hardware store. He returned to work for Doherty in 1891. Beginning in January 1895, David was starting his own hardware store in the old J. L. Welch market next to the railroad tracks. He owned this hardware store for one year, and then in 1896 joined partners with A. J. Doherty in the newly reorganized A. J.

Doherty Hardware Company. David Rorison had complete control over the operations of the store while Doherty focused his attention on the newly created Clare Wooden Ware Company.

Rorison was also involved in the political life of Clare. He served two years as the town clerk, four years as an alderman, and one two-year term (1896-1897) as the city's mayor. He left Clare in 1898 to accept a position in Saginaw with the Morley Brothers. His time in Saginaw lasted for one month when he took a position in Evart as the manager of a hardware store there. Upon leaving Clare the Rorisons rented their house to Mr. and Mrs. Haley and did not sell it until 1902.

Joseph and Lillie Worden purchased the house from the Rorisons, lived here for about five years, and sold it to Fred and Mary Ella Fishley in 1907. Before selling the house, Joseph Worden did add a new foundation and cellar.

Fred Fishley was a long time resident of Vernon Township. He moved to Vernon City in 1901, and then to a house on East Fourth Street in Clare the following year. In April 1904, Fred and his son Clarence purchased John Kirkpatrick's grocery store and operated it under the name Fred Fishley & Son. Three months later the greatest fire to occur in downtown Clare burned most of the east side of the 500 Block of North McEwan Street. Fishley's store building was a complete loss, but most of his stock of merchandise was saved. He relocated his business to his house on East Fourth Street.

In 1905, Fred joined partners with G. W. Forward in a farm produce business in the "old stand" south of the railroad tracks. Two years later the Fishley's purchased this house and only lived here for two years. Fred and Lillie obtained a divorce in 1909. Lillie moved to Mount Pleasant where she purchased the millinery business of Mrs. G. W. Forward. Fred moved to Mineral City, Ohio to live with his daughter. He passed away two years later.

Burt Greer purchased the house from the Fishley's in 1909. He married Anna Lowery in 1910. He had been married previously to Sara Orth in 1905, but the marriage ended after two weeks with Sara's death. Burt and Anna met while both of them were working at the Wm. H. Bicknell & Co. Store. They lived here until 1912 and eventually purchased the house at 805 Beech Street.

Mary Pierson bought this house from the Greers. She was the wife of the late Robert Pierson. The house was deeded to her two daughters, Jennie and Ella Pierson in 1929, with the agreement that Mary held a life lease on the house. The house was being advertised for rent starting in 1934. Ella Pierson moved to Mount Pleasant in 1935, and Jennie was again advertising the house for rent in 1941.

The house was sold to Alfred and Ortensy Cookson in 1943. Alfred originated from Clare, and married Ortensy Fleming, from Rudolph, Indiana in 1915. After their wedding, they moved to the Currie Farm located south of Clare. By 1925 they were living in Perrysburg, Ohio, and then they moved to Clare when this house was purchased. The Cooksons stayed here until 1946 and then moved to Bowling Green, Ohio.

William and Laura Karlovetz and Laura's brother Carl House purchased this house in 1947. William was born 1885, and was a retired machinist and tool and die maker before he started working as a clerk at the Doherty Hotel in 1944. William lived in this house until he passed away in 1960. Carl lived here until he died at the age of seventy-eight in 1971.

210 West Seventh Street
Constructed in 1885

John A. Jackson was born in Liverpool, England in 1858. When he was very young his parents died and he was afterward raised in a government operated orphanage. When he was eleven years old, a Catholic priest brought him along with eleven other boys and twelve girls to Canada. There he was raised by Mr. and Mrs. Caulay in the town of Frankford, Ontario.

He came to Clare in 1878. He moved for a time to the Reed City area and met and married Bridget O'Mealia. Bridget was originally from North Onslow, Quebec, and was born in 1860. John and Bridget were married in 1883 and later that same year the couple moved into the McCarty home in Sheridan Township. John's obituary stated that their first home was a log cabin in Colonville.

The family moved to Clare and built a portion of this house in 1885. John and Bridget had eight children and the house was eventually enlarged to its present size.

During the latter part of the 1880s, John was cutting trees for the Lansing Lumber Company. He continued in the lumber business until he opened his first meat market in 1894. John was a successful business man for many years. In 1903 he built a brick store building at the southeast corner of Fourth and McEwan Streets. John worked at and owned the meat market until his son Lawrence purchased the business in

John A. Jackson
Photograph from the
Forrest Meek Collection

1914. John Jackson was also involved in an automobile business in which he was partnered with his son Frank and W. J. Woodward. John retired from this in 1932.

In addition to his business activities, John served for a time as the city's third ward supervisor, and also a member of the city council. During Woodrow Wilson's presidency, he was Clare's postmaster.

Bridget Jackson lived in this house until her death in 1929. John lived here for 64 years. He passed away in 1949, just a few months short of his ninety-first birthday.

John's daughter Ethel and her husband Irwin Schleigel had moved into the house several years prior to John Jackson's death. The house stayed in the Schleigel family until the early 1970s.

215 West Seventh Street
Constructed in 1885

If awards were given to people for the most amount of years lived in one house, Anna Mussell would receive one. Her story begins with her husband Robert Mussell, who was born in 1862 and raised in Ogdensburg, New York. In 1876, he moved to the Dakotas and began work in a drugstore. He came to the Clare area in 1879 where he was employed as a bookkeeper by Ammi Wright. He married Anna Husted in 1882. Anna had lived in the Clare area since her birth in 1865. The following year Robert and Anna started their drugstore business in Clare. They first opened in the Opera House block, but later moved to the building which once stood at 515 North McEwan. Anna received her pharmacist's license in 1885.

In 1895, Robert Mussell along with Lew Davy and William Elden constructed a three storefront brick block building and moved his drug store business there. The building was located on the west side of McEwan Street between Fourth and Fifth Streets. Mussell's Drugstore was located in the center of the three storefronts and the building still stands at 505 North McEwan.

Robert died of spinal meningitis in 1902. Anna carried on the business after her husband's death until 1936, except for a period of time between 1916 and 1931, when Floyd Kirkpatrick owned the drugstore. Anna also became one of the original shareholders when the Citizens Bank became a state bank in 1909. Anna continued to act as a director of the Citizens State Bank until sometime between 1947 and 1959. She was considered by many as the most important business woman in the history of Clare.

Robert Mussell
Photograph from the
Forrest Meek Collection

This house was built in 1885 and Anna Mussell lived here until her death in 1960. She lived here a remarkable seventy-five years. During the last twelve years of her life, she was confined to her bed due to an illness which deprived her of the use of her legs. Her obituary states that despite this she had a cheerful personality.

Anna Mussell
Located on right, in front of her store
at 505 North McEwan
Photograph from the
Forrest Meek Collection

308 East Fifth Street
Constructed in 1885

Edward and Jennie White came to Clare 1883 and built this house two years later on East Fifth Street. Upon arriving in Clare, Mr. White gained employment with William Elden in the jewelry department of his bazaar business. After one year Edward White and William Elden entered into a partnership in Elden's store business. The two men worked together an additional year when Mr. White struck out on his own and located his jewelry store in the Lossing building where 515 North McEwan is now located. In 1887 Edward White constructed the current small store building at 511 North McEwan and moved his jewelry store there.

Edward and Jennie sold this house in 1890 and moved to Bay City. However, the Whites moved back to Clare at a later date. More can read be about the Whites later in this book at 114 East State Street.

During 1890 the house was sold twice, first to Joseph Nelson in February, and second to Edward and Clara Horning in August.

Edward Horning moved here from Mount Pleasant to partner with Josiah Horning in a shingle mill business. A few months later the two men made plans to leave for Akron, Ohio, and Edward sold his house to Thomas and Annie Presley. The Presleys owned a farm four miles northeast of Clare in Grant Township.

Thomas was originally from Canada and was born in 1842. He and his wife came to Clare in the late 1870s. His early years in Canada, starting at the age of twelve, were spent cutting trees in the lumber industry to provide for his family. He continued this type of employment even while living in Grant Township. His summers were spent farming while his winters were in the lumber camps.

The Presleys purchased this house in December 1890 and owned it until 1896. Upon purchasing it they began renting the house to William E. Currie. In April 1891 the Presleys moved into this house but only remained until August. Thomas Presley retained ownership of his farm in Grant Township but also traveled to various lumber camps in the winter. He rented out his house while he was away. In 1895 he was renting to J. W. Harris, and in 1896 to Mr. and Mrs. J. Horning.

Dennis and Etta Alward purchased the house toward the end of the year 1896. Dennis Alward was one of the most outstanding citizens to live in Clare. Alward started his life in Niles, Michigan, in 1859. Upon graduating from Niles Public School he attended two years of law school at the University of Michigan. Dennis got his start in the newspaper industry while working as an agent and carrier for the *Evening News* in Niles. After his days at the University of Michigan, he helped found the *Battle Creek Moon* newspaper. He came to Clare in 1879, the same year he

Dennis Alward
Photograph from the
Forrest Meek Collection

married Etta Stross and purchased the *Clare County Press* from Alvardo Goodenough. He owned the paper for eight years and changed its name to the *Clare Press* before he sold it.

Dennis Alward
Reading Clerk for the
House of Representatives
Washington D.C.
Photograph from the
Clare Sentinel 1911

After leaving the newspaper business Alward began what became a very successful political career within the Republican Party. Beginning in 1893 Alward served as the secretary of the State Senate. In 1897, the year after he purchased this house, he became the reading clerk for the United States House of Representatives in Washington D. C. He also performed the reading clerk functions at every Republican national convention from 1904 to 1928. While the House was in session Alward traveled to Washington, but when Congress was not in session he returned to his home and family in Clare. When the House of Representatives changed to Democrat control in 1911, Alward was out of a job as the House reading clerk.

After his days in Washington D. C. Alward started an insurance business located in the Citizens Bank building in 1914, and also that same year he was admitted to the state bar as a lawyer. He re-entered politics in 1914 by accepting the position of secretary of the Republican state central committee. The demands of his new position necessitated him moving to Lansing. This was done in 1917, and the house was sold to James McKay.

McKay moved to Vernon Township in 1879 along with his parents. He purchased a farm north of Clare in 1894, and soon after moved to the Detroit area where he had a very successful construction and street paving business. He never lived in this house but used it as a rental property. While reporting about a 1919 house fire in this house, the *Clare Sentinel* reported that R. A. Koch, the Standard Oil man, was living here. Later in the book the interesting life of James McKay will be continued after he purchases the house at 717 North McEwan.

James and Mary McKay sold this house to Fred Hudson, Mary's brother, in 1920. Fred and Mary's parents, Joseph and Rachel Hudson, lived in the house next door at 306 West Fifth Street. Fred Hudson was born in 1873 in Ionia, Michigan. The family soon moved to Missouri, but by the time Fred was eighteen months old his family moved back to Michigan, living on a farm in Section Two of Grant Township. He married twenty-four-year-old Alice May Evans in 1894. They purchased a farm in 1899 in the Pratt neighborhood. In addition to farming, Fred was the first rural mail carrier in Clare.

Fred Hudson
Photograph from the
Forrest Meek Collection

Starting in 1903 he delivered mail along Rural Route One and continued until he retired from the post office in 1934.

Alice's health began to decline in 1920 and the family purchased this house from James McKay in order to be closer to the help she needed. Alice passed away in 1924, and Fred married Edith Cole of Port Huron in 1928.

Although he lived in this house, Fred also rented out a portion of it. As early as 1921 he was advertising rooms for rent. Alexander Wylie was advertising his attorney and counseling services with this house as his residence in 1937. In 1940 Wylie was also advertising monthly meetings in this house as a representative of the Clare County Child Health Association.

47

After Fred retired from the post office he started in the insurance business. In addition, for a period of ten years, beginning in 1937, he served as Justice of the Peace for the City of Clare. Edith Hudson lived in this house until her death in 1948. Fred passed away in 1954 but moved out of this house and into the care of his daughter, Leah Hudson Garchow, about 1950.

209 West Seventh Street
Constructed in 1887

This house was originally constructed in 1887 as a small one-story house. It was gradually added on to, and in 1904 the second story was added. The house was built for John and Annie McDonald, who were married the previous year. John was born in 1856, in New Brunswick, Canada. He moved to Clare in 1881, where he was a lifelong lumberman.

The McDonalds resided in this house until about 1911, except for a period from 1895 to 1904 when they lived in Temple. They relocated to Roscommon in 1911 because of the greater quantity of uncut timber in the Houghton Lake area as compared to Clare.

Jay and Mary Wyman purchased this house in 1915. Jay was born in Clinton County in 1861 and married Mary Boyle in 1889. They moved to Clare in 1902.

In 1905 Jay partnered with Lyman Burch in the Burch & Wyman Grain Company. He ended his partnership with Burch in 1907, and established his own business, J. Wyman & Co., selling produce in the Geek Brothers warehouse along the railroad tracks on McEwan Street. Between 1913 and 1915 the Wyman family resided in Harrison. Jay and Mary purchased this house when they returned to Clare in 1915.

After his return to Clare, Jay worked for several years as a hay buyer. In 1915 he was responsible for shipping over 200 train cars of hay to Virginia and West Virginia. Two years later over 225 carloads of hay were shipped by him to the southern states. In 1917, when the McLaren elevator was bought out and the Clare Hay, Grain and Bean Company was constructed in its place, Jay Wyman was its first manager. It is unknown how long he worked for the firm, but in 1921, at the age of sixty, he was replaced as manager but was retained as the company's hay buyer.

Jay lived in this house until his death in 1934. After Jay's death the house was divided and an upstairs apartment was added. Mr. and Mrs. Morrel Clute were renting here in 1937, and E. R. Phinisey was renting in 1947. Their son Luman Wyman was deeded the house in 1943, with Mary having a life lease on the house. Mary passed away here in 1956. Luman, a longtime employee of both the State and County Highway Departments, owned the house until 1973.

305 East Fifth Street
Constructed in 1889

Some people might consider William Elden a little slow when it came to building this house. He purchased the lot in 1881, cleared it of stumps and graded it in 1886, and finally constructed the house in 1889.

William Elden was born near Mount Morris in the year 1849. He moved to Tittabawassee (Freeland) and met and married Mary Steckert in 1873. Mary was a native of Freeland and was born in 1855.

The Eldens came to Clare in 1875, and William promptly opened a jewelry store at 523 North McEwan. In 1883 Elden hired Ed White to work in the jewelry store, and the following year took him on as a partner. Edward White ran the jewelry portion of the business and Elden sold all the other miscellaneous items he stocked in the store. In 1885 Edward White bought out the jewelry portion

William and Mary Elden
Photographs from the Clare Sentinel 1923

of the business, and Elden went on to be famous in Clare for his bazaar store. In the early 1890s, Elden partnered with Thomas Holbrook in a bazaar store business, and this arrangement lasted until 1894. He partnered with Lew Davy and Robert Mussell in constructing a three storefront building on the west side of 500 Block of North McEwan in 1895. He moved his business into that building at 509 North McEwan that same year.

In 1902 Elden purchased A. J. Doherty's livery barn on Fourth Street and converted it into a farm implement business. A fire in 1907 burned the Fourth Street building and in the same year, he erected a new sixty-one-foot wide one-story cement block building. The building was later known as L. H. Thompson's Farm Implement Store.

William Elden retired from business in 1909. He sold his bazaar business to O. A. Derby and his son Oise in 1907. William Elden sold his building on McEwan Street to his son Norris in 1934.

Norris Elden was deeded this house in 1928 with the agreement that his parents would live there the rest of their days. Mary passed away in 1933, and William in 1939.

Prior to their deaths, the Eldens had created an apartment within the house and were renting it out. After their marriage in 1928, Kenneth and Opal Peasley were renting here. In 1933 the Herman Bell family was renting it.

After William's death, the house was purchased by Elden and Louise Roxburgh of Chicago. Elden Roxburgh was the son of William and Mary's daughter, Ethel Roxburgh. Elden and Louise owned the house until 1945 but never lived here. It is assumed they used it as a rental property. In fact, since Elden's passing, it is likely that the house has been used continuously as a rental house.

305 East Fifth Street
During William Elden's ownership
Photograph from the Robert Knapp Collection

301 East State Street
Constructed in 1891

This house was constructed in 1891 for Albert and Minnie Randall. Little is known of Albert and Minnie's past, but it is known that for a time Albert was working for the photographer E. H. DeVogt.

In 1898, the thirty-six-year-old Minnie Randall along with the baby girl she was giving birth to, passed away. Albert Randall married Lydia Plank, both of whom were born in 1858. The marriage took place prior to 1901 which was about the time they moved to Toledo.

Albert and Lydia sold the house in 1903 to John and Sarah Kirkpatrick. John was a native of Ontario who was born in 1860. From 1871 to 1872 his family moved to the Canadian Northwest before coming to Clare in 1873. While in Clare he met Sarah Badgerow, and they were married at an unknown date. John was a long time employee of the H. W. Pierce grocery store. He purchased the store from Mr. Pierce in 1903, and renamed it J. Kirkpatrick & Co.

John died at the age of forty-nine in 1909. His son Floyd, who was a clerk working for the Mussell drug store, inherited the house. Floyd resided here until 1912 when he sold it to the Clare School Superintendent Orville Poulson.

Mr. Poulson received his education from both the Ferris Institute and the Mount Pleasant Normal School. Prior to coming to Clare, he had worked in the Onekama, Augusta, and Turner School Districts. He only stayed for a few years before taking the Superintendent position at the Mesick School in 1915. A noteworthy event in his time at the Clare School was his arrest and conviction for assault and battery on a student in 1913. The case was appealed to the circuit court, but the outcome of the appeal is unknown.

Orville Poulson
Photograph from the
Clare Sentinel 1914

Henry Lydiatt owned a farm one-and-a-half miles south of Brown Corners, which he sold in 1918 and purchased this house. Henry was born in Oxfordshire, England, and moved to New York with his family at the age of fourteen. He moved to Durand, Michigan and married Mary Acker in 1886 and they moved to Clare in 1900. Henry and Mary moved out of the house in 1921 and began renting it to a Mr. Stears who was the manager of the Campbell Furniture Store. Henry died in 1923, and Mary moved into the house of her daughter and son-in-law John and Edna Coulter.

John Coulter was a native of Sheridan Township born in 1887, and Edna was born in 1884 while her family was living in Durand. They were married in 1911 and because of poor health quit farming in 1914. They acquired this house after the death of Edna's father Henry Lydiatt. After farming, John Coulter was successful in the restaurant business in Farwell, Clare and Saginaw. From 1941 until the time of his death in 1945 he was employed at the Kraft Cheese plant in Clare. It is doubtful that the Coulter's lived in the house. As early as 1925 they were advertising the house for rent. In the 1940's they had divided the house into downstairs and upstairs apartments, and were renting both.

In 1951 Edna Coulter deeded the property to her daughter and son-in-law Harold and Lucille Kigar who owned it until 1958.

305 West Sixth Street
Constructed in 1890

This house was constructed by Leonard and Emeline Hale in 1890. Little is known about the Hales. They resided in Barry County, Michigan in the 1840s, and by 1886 they were living in Iowa Falls, Iowa prior to moving to Clare at an unknown date. Emeline passed away in August 1894, and her husband Leonard followed her in death five months later.

The house was deeded to the Hale's daughter and son-in-law Mary and Henry Stevens. Henry was born in Loraine County, Ohio, in 1839. He later moved to Eaton Rapids, and while there enlisted in the Union Army serving under Captain Buck, Company F, 13th Regiment of the Michigan Infantry Volunteers. After the war, he married Mary Hale at Eaton Rapids. They moved to Clare in 1873. The Stevens built a house on East Fifth Street across from the Union Depot in 1886. He eventually converted the house to a hotel and boarding house and called it the Stevens House. While Henry owned the Stevens House, at various times he leased it to others who operated and managed it. Another business Henry operated was the moving of buildings and other large or heavy objects. In 1891 he sold this business and all the paraphernalia that went with it to Thomas Allison.

Henry and Mary's daughter was Anna Belle who married Fred Lister. The Listers are discussed later in the book for their association with the house at 813 North McEwan. The Listers moved to Millersburg, Michigan in 1900 and return in 1903. The Stevens moved to Millersburg in 1902 and also returned in 1903.

The Stevens most likely rented out their house while they were gone because on their return they took up residence at the Exchange Hotel. Mary Stevens passed away in 1908 while living here. Henry moved out sometime before 1910 and rented the house to Mr. and Mrs. William Roof.

As mentioned earlier, Henry Stevens owned the Stevens House on Fifth Street. The Stevens House was located on the lot immediately to the south of this house. The Stevens House burned down sometime between 1900 and 1906. The following story was reported in the June 10, 1910, issue of the *Clare Sentinel*, and relates a near fatal incident at the former Stevens House site.

On Tuesday afternoon the two children of Wm. Roof, living on West 6th street of this city had a very narrow escape from drowning.

It seems the two girls aged 4 and 6 years respectively left the house to gather "Sweet Mary" in a vacant lot on which the old Stevens House formerly stood and which is directly back of Mr. Roof's place. In the lot is the old cistern used by the hotel in days gone by. The cistern has no covering, is entirely open, and water to the depth of five feet stands in it. It is hidden from view by tall grass, which has grown around it. The youngest child came running along and fell into the cistern. The oldest girl seeing her little sister fall into the cistern, jumped in to save her.

Seeing perhaps that she could not save her sister, she managed to crawl out by some unknown and unaccountable way and immediately ran to the house, dripping with water and notified her mother by exclaiming, "Ma! Ma! little sister has fallen in a big river." The mother was washing at the time. The little girl took her mother's hand and guided her to the cistern and pointed in and said: "Baby sister in there!" The mother frantic with grief, jumped in to rescue her baby while the girl ran to the union depot and called help. A number of men from the depot ran to the spot where a pitiful sight was witnessed. There stood the loving mother in water up to her shoulders holding her darling baby in her arms above her head. The mother and child were rescued and the baby taken to the house when Dr. Sanford and Dr. F. R. Gray were called, and by using artificial respiration and rolling the baby over a barrel the water was removed from its lungs. From latest reports, the child will live and no bad results are apt to occur from its experience, but nevertheless, the party or parties who own this vacant lot should be compelled by law to place a covering over the cistern. In fact, they should be punished as it is for not covering this treacherous hole.

The next year Henry Stevens constructed a new dwelling house at the location of the old Stevens House, thus taking care of the "treacherous hole."

The 305 West Sixth Street house was sold by Henry Stevens to Mary Boyd in 1910. Mary owned the house until 1914 when she sold it to Florence Dunwoodie. Florence sold the house to Harvey and Ada Erter in 1918, and they owned it until the end of the decade.

The year 1920 saw Frank and Maude Holmes making this house their home. Frank was born in Allen County, Ohio, in 1885, and Maude Bowen was born in 1889, in Isabella County. Frank was a long time employee of the Pere Marquette and C & O Railroads.

He worked as a telegraph operator in the Union Depot Tower. By 1938 the house was being advertised for rent.

The Holmes divorced in 1942, and Maude was deeded the house. She retained ownership of it, and rented it until 1945. In that year, Dr. Harmon and Virginia Ballard purchased the house, and continued to use it as a rental property. They owned it until the 1980s.

There are only two known renters from the mid-twentieth century. The first is Norman and Marjorie Jackson who rented in the mid-1940s. Norman at the age of thirty was receiving his naval indoctrination training at Great Lakes, Illinois in 1945.

The second renter was Russell Thurston, who rented for a short time in the early 1950s. Russell owned the Thurston Funeral Home at 114 West Fifth Street. In 1951 there was an explosion in that building. The damage was extensive enough that Thurston needed to relocate both his residence and his business. This house served both functions for one year until Russell could build a new facility for his funeral home business.

101 Maple Street
Constructed in 1891

Charles Lewis Brown was born in 1820 in Rochester, New York. At the age of 24, he married Sarah Evans, who was born in 1821 and was also from the state of New York. About 1843 the family moved to Ionia County, Michigan, and twenty years later to Mount Pleasant. They moved to Clare in 1891 and built this house.

The house was sold to Martha Bicknell in 1899, with the consideration that Charles and Sarah had a life lease on the property. Charles passed away in December of that year. Martha Bicknell deeded the property to her son James in 1902, continuing the life lease of Sarah Brown. Sarah passed away later that year.

James and Alberta Bicknell moved into this house in October 1902, one month after Sarah Brown's death. The lives of James and Alberta Bicknell will not be discussed here, but more will be shared about them later in the book at 113 West Fifth Street.

James Bicknell
Photograph from the
Forest Meek Collection

The Bicknells sold the house to Clyde and Edith Holliday in 1914. The Hollidays came from Indiana in 1909 and settled on a farm about one mile north of Clare. It seems that Clyde simultaneously sold his farm and purchased this house. They lived in this house for less than a year but did not sell the house until 1918.

James and Annie Arrand purchased this house from the Hollidays. The Arrands were both originally from Canada. James was born in 1858 in Ontario, and Annie Lowery was born in Hastings County, Ontario in 1867. James arrived in Clare around 1882, and Annie moved here about three years later. They were married in 1886. James was a building contractor but was also known for raising and moving buildings. James died in 1924, and Annie lived on until 1945.

After Annie's death, the house was sold to Lloyd and Minnie Edick. Lloyd was born in Gladwin County in 1888. He married Geneva Perron, also from Gladwin, in 1910. It is unknown when Lloyd and Geneva came to Clare, but Lloyd was working as a hardware purchaser for the Clare Hardware and Furniture Company starting about 1919. Lloyd and Geneva divorced in 1927, and Lloyd married Minnie Zimmerman in 1929. Minnie was a lifelong resident of Clare County and was born in 1908. Lloyd passed away at the age of fifty-nine in 1947.

Lloyd and Minnie had one son, Lloyd Jr. Lloyd Jr. was a veteran of the Korean War. He served with the 8206th Army Unit in 1953. His job was to furnish supplies, transportation, communications, and services to UN fighting forces. The following year, with the war over, Lloyd Jr. was working for the City of Clare. The following story was taken from the September 3, 1954, issue of the *Clare Sentinel*:

Lloyd a City employee was at work laying a piece of tile in the new sewage system being constructed in the northwest part of town.

About 9:30 am. Monday, Edick along with Bill Barber an engineering student, doing summer work for the city in the sewerage project went down into the ditch.

Above them, a large crane stood idle with the crane operator, Don Walker waiting to continue the tile laying operations. Other city employees were at work at the other end of the ditch, about 100 feet away.

Edick upon reaching the bottom of the cut began shifting the tile into position. Barber was standing a few feet from him.

Barber told how they first noticed a trickle of sand fall from the opposite side of the ditch. Suddenly, the fall increased until it was with some effort that he (Barber) was able to move his feet.

Then, Barber said he heard Edick shout, 'Look out, get out of here.'

Barber leaped aside feeling a heavy object brush his leg. Edick stood as though frozen as a huge three-ton catch basin fell on his body.

The basin had been lodged above at the top of the ditch where men had dug around it. According to workmen, the basin had been in that position since the week end.

The basin pinned Edick against the side of the ditch. Workmen rushed to his side in an attempt to dig him out. The attempt failed. As the basin fell away from its position, it broke off a water main and the water flooded the rescue area making the digging difficult.

Soon it was found that the only way to get Edick out was to lift the basin from him using the crane. Meanwhile, about ten minutes had passed since the huge brick and iron object had fallen lodging itself against him.

Ten minutes later, after several heartbreaking attempts, the basin was slowly lifted from Edick.

At ten o'clock he was taken to Clare General Hospital. There doctors immediately declared his position as "very critical." It was later learned that he suffered from multiple fractures of legs and back.

An hour and ten minutes later at 11:10 his condition was the same and doctors were treating him for "shock." Little hope was held out for his recovery and 40 minutes later he was dead.

Workmen at the scene of the accident broke down upon the death of the young man they had tried so hard to save.

This is the first time in the modern history of the city that one of its employees had been killed in the line of duty.

Lloyd Jr.'s mother, Minnie, continued to live in this house until her death in 1968.

104 West State Street
Constructed in 1891

James F. Tatman was born in Nicholsville, Clermont County, Ohio, on March 25, 1859. At the age of five his family moved to Indiana, and then to Clare County in 1878. Upon arriving he found a job teaching at the Dover School, and later in the Eagle and Colonville Schools.

Two years after settling in Clare County he married Lizzie Alina Berry.

Lizzie was born on December 13, 1862 in Elmira, New York. Her father, William Berry, died while fighting in the Civil War that same year. Her mother remarried and the family moved to Isabella County in 1870.

James and Lizzie moved to Clare in 1882. He was first employed in the Nathan Bicknell and Company store. Two years later he formed a partnership with J. H. Schilling, and in 1885 he went into the grocery business for himself, locating in the Callaghan building. Tatman eventually relocated his store to the east side of the 500 block of North McEwan. The great fire of July 1904 burned the wood frame structure where his business was located and Tatman replaced it with the present brick building located at 506 North McEwan. James and George McKeever formed a business partnership starting in 1905. Mr. McKeever purchased a half interest in the Tatman grocery business, and Tatman obtained a half interest in the McKeever sawmill business. This partnership lasted until 1913. At that time, Tatman's son, James A. Tatman, became a partner in the grocery business. James F. Tatman retired from the grocery business in 1930.

James F. Tatman
Photograph from the
Clare Sentinel 1937

James also served as a director and officer of the Retail Grocers and Meat Dealers Association of Michigan, was a director of the Clare Chamber of Commerce, and a member of the Clare Board of Education.

This house was constructed in 1891. Lizzie passed away in 1906, and James remarried in 1920. His new wife Drucilla was an old friend of his former wife. Drucilla had been widowed from her husband, Charles S. Chase, since his death in 1900. Drucilla passed away in 1935 and James followed her in death two years later in 1937.

After his death, James' three children, Alina Andrus, James A. Tatman, and Elva Tatman, all inherited an interest in the house. Elva was preceded in death by James A. and Alina and retained ownership of the house until her death, at the age of seventy-four, in 1963. Elva was a graduate of the Mount Pleasant Normal School and later Columbia University. She was employed as a dietitian with the Baltimore Maryland School system and spent her summers at the family home on State Street.

206 West Seventh Street
Constructed in 1891

Warren and Adella Keller had this house built in 1891. It is unknown where or when Warren was born, but he lived in Epsilon, Emmet County, prior to arriving in Clare. Warren and Adella were married in 1885. She was born in 1865 and originated from Crawford County, Pennsylvania. She departed this life in September 1895 at the age of thirty-one. An event that caused her husband Warren to leave Clare and return to Epsilon a few months later.

Prior to Warren's departure from Clare, Frederick Lister began renting the Keller house. He purchased the property in 1897. The life of Fred Lister will be discussed later in the book for the house at 813 North McEwan Street.

Fred Lister left Clare for a period of about five years starting in 1900. Edward and Louise Waller purchased the house from Lister, but the research is conflicting as to when it happened.

Edward Waller was born in 1866 in Frankfort, Ontario. He came to Clare in 1887, working as a clerk in a lumbering camp. He married Louise Weeks in 1892. In August 1891, he started in the boot and shoe business with Henry Razek and was located in the Opera House block. The business was relocated the next month to the Theo Boge building (517 North McEwan). By the end of the year 1892, Edward Waller had bought out the business interest of Henry Razek and was in business for himself. Waller purchased the Theo Boge building in 1894 and continued in business there until 1905, when he relocated to Gladwin.

Here is where the matter of when Edward Waller purchased this house comes into question. A *Clare Courier* article from April 24, 1903, reports "Ed. H. Waller has this week purchased the Fred Lister residence property on West Seventh Street and will occupy it shortly."

The *Clare Sentinel* wrote on June 16, 1905, just prior to Waller leaving for Gladwin, "Geo. E. Hersey has purchased the E. H. Waller residence on Seventh Street." The following year Edward Waller returned to Clare from Gladwin, but there is no record of him purchasing the house he previously owned back from Hersey. In fact, on his return to Clare, the newspaper states that the Wallers rented a house from Maynard on Seventh Street (most likely 313 or 315 East Seventh). It's not until 1907 that the paper reports twice about Edward Waller purchasing a house on Seventh Street. The second report states that he is adding a "porch of stone" to the residence. The Sanborn Maps shows a different porch on the 1910 map than was shown on the 1906 map. To further confuse things the deed for the sale of the property from Fred Lister to Edward Waller is dated 1909.

John Blanken purchased the property from the Wallers in March 1915. He and his family were only in Clare for less than a year due to John's poor health. John Blanken sold his bakery business in October and the next month left for Grand Rapids.

In 1915 the house was sold to Dr. Joseph and Nora Roe. Dr. Roe came to Clare from Portland to take over the dental practice of Dr. Neeland, who lived at 604 Pine Street. Joseph Roe was a graduate of Northwestern University, Chicago, and located his business in the Elden Block at 509 North McEwan Street. Dr. Roe left Clare in 1922 when his practice was purchased by Dr. Frank McKnight.

Although Dr. Roe left Clare in 1922, his house was not sold to Sheral and Maude Callihan until 1931. Sheral was from Sandusky County, Ohio, and was born in 1888. In 1910 he married Maude Porterfield in Alma. They came to Clare in 1921, and Sheral immediately went into the real estate business. His office was located in the building on the southeast corner of McEwan and Fifth Streets. In 1931 he relocated his office to the building formerly occupied by Clare Realty Company.

The Callihans sold the house in 1938 to Lyle and Josephine

Dr. Joseph Roe
Photograph from the
Clare Sentinel 1911

Chapman. Lyle was a native of Akron, Michigan, and was born in 1897. Josephine Haynak was born in 1903 in Hungary. They were married in 1921 in Lansing, Michigan. The Chapmans came to Clare in 1935, when Lyle and his brother-in-law Frank Haynak opened the Clare Auto Parts Store on West US-10 near the County Road Commission Building. The business relocated in 1936 to downtown in the newly erected addition on the west end of 427 North McEwan Street. Lyle passed away in 1944 at the age of forty-six.

After Lyle's death, Josephine re-entered the work force and opened a restaurant. In 1953 she purchased the Thomas Lunch business across from the Clare Manufacturing Company on West US-10. She had experience working in the restaurant business while living in Mount Morris ten years prior to moving to Clare. Ten years later, in 1963, she was advertising the business for sale.

Josephine lived in this house until she sold it in 1968. She enjoyed twenty-four more years of life in Clare before she passed away in 1992.

206 West Seventh Street
Circa 1920s
Photograph from the Robert Knapp Collection

212 West State Street
Constructed in 1891

Byron Alger was born in 1846 in Colburn, Ontario. In 1862 he left Canada and moved with his family to Minnesota. The family returned to Canada and then returned to the United States, this time settling in St. Claire County, Michigan. Along with his brother, Henry, they joined Company H, First Connecticut; Heavy Artillery, and were assigned to the Army of the Potomac. He was honorably discharged in October 1865 and moved back to St. Claire County with his brother.

Two years later Byron, along with his brother and his father purchased eighty acres of farm land in section fifteen of Vernon Township. In 1875 Byron married Eva Ledsworth from St. Claire County. Eva passed away in 1877. He remarried in 1880 to Maggie Murdock, who passed away in 1881. 1883 saw Byron marrying Jennie Greenway.

Jennie's birth name was Ann Jane Robinson, and she was born in 1851 in Ontario, Canada. In 1869 she married G. H. Greenway also of Ontario, Canada. Mr. Greenway passed away in 1876 and Jennie moved to Clare shortly after his death.

Byron purchased his father's farm in 1875 and farmed there for many years. By 1895 he had replaced farming for carpentry as his main occupation. He built this house in 1891 and sold it to Hugh McKinnon in 1905. It is possible the exterior of the house was altered later because the brickwork is more mid-twentieth century in appearance than late-nineteenth century.

Hugh McKinnon was born in 1842 in Conington, Ontario. In the 1860s he married Rachel Shier from Brock, Ontario, who was five years his senior. They moved to Michigan about 1883. They first made their home in Loomis, and then two years later purchased an eighty-acre farm in section sixteen of Sheridan Township. Because both were suffering ill health, Hugh and Rachel quit farming and purchased this house in Clare. Rachel passed away at the home of her daughter Margaret Bulman in 1906 and Hugh also died in 1908.

Margaret and her husband Amos Bulman were deeded this property after the death of Hugh McKinnon. The Bulman's owned the house until 1917 when it was sold to Lawrence Jackson.

Lawrence Jackson was a lifelong citizen of Clare. He was born to John and Bridget Jackson in 1884. In 1907 he married Josephine Cour, who was born in Saginaw in 1882. A 1898 newspaper article had Josephine working as the "new telephone girl and bookkeeper" at the A. J. Doherty & Son's Store. A 1907 article mentions her as a phone operator for the Bell Company. Lawrence worked in his father's meat market at the southeast corner of Fourth and McEwan Streets and purchased it in 1914. His son Lawrence Jr. bought the business from him in 1955. Josephine lived in this house until she passed away in 1959, and Lawrence lived here until his death in 1965.

307 East Fifth Street
Constructed in 1891

Martha Bogardus was an early business woman in Clare. She was born Martha Brady, in 1845, being a native of Ontario, Canada. She married Cornelius Bogardus in 1867; he died in 1903. Martha came to Clare in 1873, but there is no mention of her husband joining her. In fact, the newspapers only mention a C. E. Bogardus twice. The first is in connection to a C. E. Bogardus from Chicago selling liquor illegally in Eldorado Kansas in 1890. It is likely that this is not the C. E. Bogardus that was married to Martha. However, the second mention states a C. E. Bogardus was in Clare in 1902 in the interest of the International Business College of Saginaw. This is the only information we might have on Martha Bogardus' husband.

Martha came to Clare in 1873 and started a millinery store located in a building she owned on McEwan Street. The May 28,

1878, issue of the *Clare County Press* states the building was located on the next street north of the Stearns House. She built this house in 1891 and lived in it until she passed away in 1910.

For one year after Martha's death, the house was rented to Clarence Geek. In 1911 Simon Bogardus, Martha Bogardus' son, along with his family moved from his house at 210 East State Street to this house.

Simon Bogardus was born in St. Catherines, Ontario, in 1870. He came to Clare with his mother in 1873. He married Eva Harris in 1893. She was a native of Amherstburg, Ontario, and was born the same year as Simon. She came to Clare with her family when she was ten years old.

When he was a young man, Simon Bogardus started his employment in the grocery business of Tatman & Schilling. In 1895 he purchased the Albert Smith interest of the Smith & Ritter meat market, and the business was renamed, Ritter & Bogardus. Simon and Harvey Ritter dissolved their partnership in 1897. It is assumed that Simon went back to work in James Tatman's grocery store because the next mention of his employment is in 1900 when he quit his job with Tatman. The following year Simon Bogardus started his own grocery business. For a time after 1910 and until 1916, he was leasing the south unit of the Dunwoodie building at 601 North McEwan. In 1916 he constructed the brick building at 513 North McEwan and operated his store out of there. In 1920 Bogardus partnered with Norris Elden and Fred Thompson in a men's and boys clothing store. The business stayed open until 1924 when it was bought out by the Wilson-Davy Company. Simon continued to work at his grocery business until his retirement in 1929.

Simon Bogardus passed away in 1941. Eva Bogardus sold the house in 1945 and moved in with her daughter, Hilda Tibbils, at 211 East Sixth Street until her death in 1956.

Marvin Witbeck purchased the house from Eva Bogardus. Marvin came to Clare in 1935 from Evart to manage the Kroger Grocery and Baking Company's newly opened store. The store was located in the south unit of 524 North McEwan. The store location was the former home of the Clare Post Office. Kroger stayed in this location until 1939, when it moved to the old Clare County Savings Bank on the southwest corner of Fourth and McEwan Streets. Marvin continued to manage the Kroger store until August of 1946 when he was transferred for three months to the Mount Pleasant Kroger store. He continued to live at his Clare house on East Fifth Street while he was working in Mount Pleasant.

Marvin Witbeck
Photograph from the
Forrest Meek Collection

Marvin returned to the Clare Store in November 1946. In 1948 Kroger opted to relocate to a new building farther west on Fourth Street. At that time, Marvin along with his brother Rolland started the Witbeck IGA Store in the former Kroger store building on the corner of Fourth and McEwan Streets. Rolland sold his interest in

307 East Fifth Street
Unknown Date
Photograph from the
Forrest Meek Collection

the store in 1950. A fire in 1957, which destroyed most of the block south of the Witbeck store, was motivation for Marvin to relocate to the north of Clare's downtown and at the same time triple the size of his store.

Marvin Witbeck continued to live at this house until at least the mid-1950s.

310 West Wheaton Avenue
Constructed in 1891

From tax records, it has been determined that this house was constructed in 1891. The first owner of the house was Amanda Ross. From the newspaper research, there was no one by the name of Amanda Ross that lived in Clare. However, the mother of local store owner William Ross, who came to Clare in 1872, was named Amanda. There is no other known Amanda Ross with connections to Clare, so it is quite possible this is the correct Amanda Ross.

Mrs. Ross was born in 1819, in Cayuga County, New York. She married the twenty-three-year-old Giles Ross in 1839. They came to Michigan in 1863 and settled in Highland, Michigan, in Livingston County. Giles was elected to the Michigan House of Representatives in 1872 and served two terms until 1876. The name Amanda Ross is also associated with the ownership of a boarding house in Clare at 114 West Fifth Street from 1886 to 1895. Giles passed away in 1892; Amanda departed this life in 1902.

After Byron and Jennie Alger sold their house at 212 West State Street in 1905, they purchased this house the following year. For the year after he sold the house on State Street until he purchased this house, he and his wife Jennie lived in the Beemer residence on North McEwan Street. This house was likely a retirement home for the Algers since Byron was sixty years old when they moved here. Jennie Alger lived here until her death in 1923; Byron passed away in 1929.

The house was not sold until 1936 when Arthur and Augusta Morgan purchased it. Prior to this, a Mr. and Mrs. R. I. Hether were living here, but it is unknown when they moved in.

Arthur Morgan was originally from Ionia, Michigan, being born there in 1882. He married Augusta in 1931 and moved to Clare from Sault Ste. Marie in 1934. It is doubtful if they ever lived in this house. Almost immediately after purchasing the house the Morgans started to advertise that it was for rent. The Morgans most likely lived in an apartment at the Clare Inn. The Inn was located at 115 West Fourth Street and had previously gone by the names of the Lackie House and Central Hotel. The Morgans who started managing the inn in 1937 purchased it in 1941, and continued its operation until it was torn down in 1959 to make room for a parking lot for Witbeck's grocery store.

Arthur and Augusta Morgan sold this house to Arthur and Louise Grosvenor in 1945. Prior to moving into this house, they owned a cattle ranch in Wise Township. Arthur was also a long time railroad worker. Starting in 1910, Grosvenor was a section laborer for the C. & N. W. railroad in Telon, South Dakota. Eight years later he was an employee of the Ann Arbor Railroad in Cohoctah, Michigan. In 1919 he switched to the Pere Marquette Railroad and served as an operator in Coleman, Baldwin, Scottville, and Flint. He came to Clare in 1922, where he worked as a tower operator. Several months after purchasing this house in 1945 he was named the station agent.

The Grosvenors were married in 1908 and had eight children. One of their sons, Robert, served in the First Infantry

Division (the Big Red One) in the European Command in the early 1950s. Louise Grosvenor passed away while living in this house in 1948. Arthur moved out of the house in 1951 and moved to Duarte, California.

The house was sold to Leo and Mamie Heintz in 1954 and then again to Paul and Elva Lapham in 1959.

805 Beech Street
Constructed in 1891

Frank Grover was a single man when he built this house in 1891. This is one of eight houses featured in this book that was built in that year. Grover was born in 1859 and originated from Tuscola County. After moving with his family to Oakland County he came to the Clare area in 1883. He married Eliza Lowry, who was from Clare, in 1895. In addition to this house, he also owned a farm three miles north of Clare, which he farmed for twenty years. In the early 1890s, Grover supplemented his income by going into partnership with Dave Wood and purchased a threshing machine. They hired out the threshing machine to local farms. Later in 1903, Grover purchased his own new fifteen horsepower Case threshing machine.

Grover sold this house in 1915 and moved to a farm just outside of the village of Marion. He sold this house to Burt and Ann

Burt Greer
*Photograph from the
Clare Sentinel 1905*

Greer the following year. Burt Greer was a native of Gladwin. He began work in the Bicknell Company store in Shepherd in 1899. In 1902 he came to work at the William H. Bicknell and Company dry goods and clothing store in Clare. Burt married Ann Lowery of Clare, in 1910. Burt ended up spending fifty years of his employable life working at the Bicknell's store.

Burt Greer died in 1952. His wife Ann survived him until 1977, living in this house for sixty-two years.

1005 North McEwan Street
Constructed in 1891

William H. Goodman was born in Detroit in 1832. He was the son of a Baptist minister and moved quite frequently around southeastern Michigan when he was a youth. When he was an adult he lived in Troy until moving to Birmingham in 1867. William married Rachel Rockafellow in 1856. Rachel was born in Mount Morris, New York, in 1834, and was living in Atlas, Michigan, when they were wed.

William served as the postmaster while living in Troy and on the Board of Education while in Birmingham. The family came to Clare in 1882. Upon their arrival, William and his son William A. Goodman went into the hardware business on the south end of McEwan Street, purchasing the hardware business of John Calkins before he moved to Arizona. The father and son partnership was dissolved in 1897 and the business sold to William H. Goodman's son John. William and Rachel built this house in 1891 and William lived here until his death in 1900.

Rachel continued to live in the house after William's passing. Starting in 1901 she began renting out rooms in the house. The list of people renting from her is a regular who's who of Clare citizens. A list of known renters is as follows; C. H. VanBrunt (1901), Herman Rogers and his mother (1904), Frank Louch (1905), Mr. and Mrs. A. J. Lacy (1908-1909), Mr. and Mrs. Lee Dunwoodie (1909), D. Willis (1911), B. H. Demarest and family (1915), W. E. Vance (1916), and newlyweds Rollie and Loretta Lytle (1918).

Rachel passed away in 1923 and the house was deeded to her one remaining son John R. Goodman. John was born in 1864 when the Goodman family was living in Troy. He worked in his father's hardware store after moving to Clare. He worked for two years as a bookkeeper for a local lumber company before moving to Loomis to construct a general store and served as postmaster. He returned to Clare in 1897 to take over his father's and brothers' hardware store.

John R. Goodman
Photograph from the
Clare Courier 1903

In 1903 John R. Goodman was one of the original founders along with Fred Lister, George Benner, and C. H. O'Donald, of the Citizens Bank. He served the Citizens Bank as assistant cashier for twenty years. From 1927 to 1929 he was elected to the position of cashier for the State Bank of Mackinac Island. He returned to Clare in 1929 because of ill health and passed away while living in this

82

house in 1933. John R. Goodman was such a respected citizen that the new street constructed in 1937, which was located one block north of Wheaton Avenue and ran west from McEwan Street, was named "John R. Street" in his honor.

During John Goodman's period of poor health, his nephew Fred Goodman and Fred's wife Daisley moved into this house to care for him. Fred and Daisley inherited the house after John's death. Fred was born in 1887, the son of John's brother William Goodman. After graduating from Clare Public Schools he attended the Saginaw Business College where he studied accounting. He later married Daisley Inman in Chicago, made their home there, and eventually moved to Detroit.

Daisley was born in 1888 in Bellevue, Michigan. Her father passed away after her graduation from Bellevue High School, and she moved with her mother to Battle Creek. While in Battle Creek she worked for several years as a buyer for the Schroeder Brothers Dry Goods Store.

When Fred and Daisley lived in Chicago and Detroit, Fred was employed as an accountant by the Austin Company which caused him to travel extensively throughout the country. The Goodmans even resided for a time in Astoria, Oregon, while working for the Austin Company. Fred also worked as an accountant for the United States Government during World War I. Fred and Daisley moved to Clare about 1925 and remained here after that. By 1946 they were operating The Manor Inn out of this house.

Both Fred and Daisley passed away in 1948. The house was purchased the following year by Carl Stephenson, and he converted it to the Stephenson Funeral Home. Carl Stephenson located here from Flint,

Carl Stephenson
Photograph from the
Forrest Meek Collection

83

but he had roots in Clare. His grandfather was the late L. H. Thompson and Carl's wife was the former Virginia Poet from Sheridan Township.

Stephenson Funeral Home
With their new 1949 Packards on display
Photograph from the Forrest Meek Collection

303 East State Street
Constructed in 1892

Thomas Naylor constructed this house in 1892. Other than he was a long time employee of the Clare Hardware Company, little is known about him. He sold this house in 1897 to George and Katherine McKeever in order to relocate and open his own hardware store in Gladwin.

George McKeever was originally from Livingston County, where he was born in 1859. He moved to Isabella County in 1876 and then to Clare in 1893. Upon arriving in Clare, George, along with Fred Hubel and Peter McKeever, refitted the Hubel grist mill, just west of the union depot into a shingle mill. The mill employed fifteen men and cut 25,000 shingles a day. By the next year, McKeever was desiring to build a new mill in Clare, but that would not come to be until 1896. In that year McKeever formed a

Katherine and George McKeever
Photograph from Clare Remembered

partnership with C. H. O'Donald and they constructed a shingle mill just west of Lamb's mill.

In 1889, George McKeever married Katherine McKeever (it is unknown if they were related). Katherine was born in Edenville, Michigan, in 1872. She lived in both Isabella County and Harrison and taught one year at a rural school.

George and Katherine lived in this house until 1902. That year he purchased the building on the corner of Sixth and McEwan Streets and moved his family into the rooms on the second floor. The building was described as the location of

W. D. Riggs
Photograph from the Forrest Meek Collection

86

Willoughby's Photography. He rented 303 East State Street for one year to W. D. Riggs, who was the Clare School Superintendent. The following year George made arrangements with David R. Johnson for a trade of properties. George gave David Johnson his two properties on East State Street (210 and 303) in exchange for Johnson's farm in Grant Township. David Johnson's health was failing and he needed to quit farming. At the same time, George and Katherine purchased the house at 106 West Wheaton and moved there immediately.

In 1904, with presumably improved health, David Johnson did another property trade. This time he traded 303 East State Street for the Levi Montney Farm located on Dover Road. Mr. Montney was born in 1844, in Jefferson County, New York. He enlisted in the Union Army in 1864 and came to Clare County in 1880. After the death of his wife Fanny in 1904, he gave up farming and moved into this house. Montney formed a partnership with B. F. Loomis, in 1907, to manufacture cement tiles and culverts in Clare.

Levi Montney sold his house to Frank and Minnie Lamoreaux in 1912, and they sold it the next year to Julius and Caroline Schug.

Julius Schug was a long-time farmer in Vernon Township just west of Stevenson Lake. He was born in Ulmet, Germany in 1851. He immigrated to America at the age of twenty-one and settled in Syracuse, New York. He returned to Germany in 1881 for a short stay. Julius came back to Syracuse the next year accompanied by the twenty-three-year-old Caroline Drumm, who was also from Ulmet, Germany. After returning to Syracuse, Julius and Caroline were married. The Schugs moved to their farm in Vernon Township two weeks after their marriage in 1882. They farmed there for thirty years, and just prior to retirement they planned a visit to their homeland for the Drumm family reunion. When it came time to return to America, Caroline became ill enough that they could not travel. It's usually not said that becoming ill is a good thing, but strangely in this instance, it was. By delaying their return trip until Caroline was well, the Schugs were not able to use their tickets for their return trip on the Titanic. The Titanic famously sank on April 15, 1912.

They purchased this house in 1913 and Julius lived here until his passing in 1933. In 1943, because of ill health, Caroline sold this house and moved in with her daughter. She passed away the following year.

The house was sold to Joseph Hendrie, who used it as a rental property. Hendrie, born in 1864 in Rockton, Ontario, Canada, located to the Farwell area at the age of fifteen. Joseph married Sarah Solen in 1887 and they later moved to her parent's farm in Vernon Township. The farm was located on Stevenson Lake and the Hendrie's founded Hendrie Landing there.

Joseph retired in 1911 and moved into a house on East Fifth Street. The only known renters he had was the Earl Patton family. They rented from 1944 to 1946. At the time he lived here Earl was a title man for the Sohio Petroleum Company. Joseph Hendrie owned the house until his death in 1959.

210 East State Street
Constructed in 1893

This house was constructed for C. P. Louch in 1893. Little is known about C. P. Louch, even what C. P. stands for. However, we do know that he was Clare City Clerk for many years during the 1890s. He was also a salesman at A. J. Doherty's hardware store, starting in 1895 after David Rorison left the firm.

C. P. Louch began renting his house to Henry Alger in 1898 while Louch moved his family to Manistee. He returned to Clare and this house in 1901.

George and Katherine McKeever purchased this property in 1902, presumably as an investment property. The following year McKeever sold this house along with the one at 303 East State Street to David Johnson. As you will remember, David Johnson was ill and needed to quit farming to regain his health. The following year he sold both of his houses on East State Street. Johnson sold this house to Simon and Eva Bogardus.

The Bogardus family lived here until 1911 when they moved into his mother's, Martha Bogardus', home at 307 East Fifth Street. We have already discussed Simon and Eva's life in that narrative and will not go over it again here.

The Bogardus' sold this home to Lester and Lillie Fox. Lester Fox was born in 1878, in North Star Township, Gratiot County. His father died when he was at a very young age and his mother and stepfather were killed in a railroad accident while still in his youth. He was raised by an uncle for several years. His first wife died after being married for a short time. His second wife was named Lilly Stone; they had one child that died in infancy just before they arrived in Clare.

Prior to living in Clare, Lester Fox worked in the lumber business in North Star, resided in Montana for a time for health reasons, and lived in St. Louis where he learned the jewelry and watch business. Lester and Lilly moved to Clare in 1910 and purchased the jewelry business of C. J. Grill which was located in the Jackson Block. The year after the Foxs moved to Clare they purchased this home. Lester died at the early age of thirty-seven in 1915. His wife Lilly married Winn Bartram of Detroit in 1919 and moved there.

In 1919, the house was deeded to a trio of women, Olive, Leslie and Ruth Stone. They were likely related to Lilly Fox, since her maiden name was Stone. The newspapers mention Olive and Ruth, but not Leslie. Nothing is reported of any of the three women in connection to this house.

Fred and Florence Newsom purchased the house in 1921. Fred was from Eagle in Clinton County and was born in 1863. When he was a young adult he began work in a dry goods store in Grand Ledge. He stayed in Grand Ledge for nine years and then moved to Boyne City, where he worked twelve years in a harness shop. He later moved to Ubly and continued the same line of work.

When the Newsoms came to Clare in 1920, Fred set up a vulcanizing shop at 515 North McEwan in Clare's downtown. He later added battery sales to his line of work. The year after he started his business in Clare he purchased this house on State Street. He passed away in April 1931; by July of the same year Florence was renting out the house and most likely living in another portion of it. It has been a rental property ever since.

In 1934, Florence traded this house with Ida Crigier for Ida's two-family apartment house on West Sixth Street. Like Florence, Ida may have lived in part of the house and rented the rest. An article in the 1942 newspaper reports on Wallace Crigier, Ida's son, who lived at this address, as going to Naval Training School for electricians at the University of Minnesota.

Ida sold the house in 1945 to Thomas and Mainie Mae Hysell. The Hysells owned the house until 1950 when they sold it to Doris Grant. A. T. Carrow purchased the house from Doris Grant and owned it into the mid-1950s.

The known renters for this house are: Mr. and Mrs. Delbert Nolan mid-1940s, Mrs. C. A. Urquhart mid to late 1940s, Don Kirkpatrick late 1940s, and L. C. Bird mid-1950s.

The May 5, 1944, issue of the *Clare Sentinel* reported that Delbert Nolan Jr, the nineteen-month-old son of Mr. and Mrs. Delbert Nolan, fell out of a second story window of this house, onto the cement sidewalk below, and miraculously survived. Although he suffered from shock and some bruises, he had no broken bones. He was treated by Dr. F. C. Sanford of Clare and Dr. William L. Harrigan of Mount Pleasant and released.

618 North Rainbow Drive
Constructed in 1893

Dr. J. H. Johnson came to Clare in 1892. He was a veterinarian who received his education at the Ontario Veterinary College in Toronto. After coming to Clare, he initially set up his office in Parrish's livery barn. He built this house in 1893 but later left for the town of Ewen in the western Upper Peninsula. He returned in 1895 and left again the following year to setup a practice in Ohio.

The house was sold to David Clark in 1896. He had a number of jobs while living in Clare. For the most part, he was a railroad worker. For a number of years he worked as the express man for the American Express Co., a position he resigned from in 1903. He was also the owner of an ice house. A 1903 *Clare Sentinel* advertisement stated that he had a stock of 800 tons of ice. Clark sold the ice house business to the Clare Ice and Coal Company in 1903. Clark was also a drayman for the railroad, which he worked at until he moved to Detroit in 1906.

David Clark eventually sold his house, but not until 1909. James and Louise Armstrong were the next owners of the house. James was born in Calladen, Ontario, in 1844. James settled in Vernon Township in 1869. He married Louise Hinds in 1876, who was from Stanton, Michigan. They moved to Farwell and settled on land originally owned by Louise's parents. They lived on the farm until they purchased this house in Clare. James and Louise lived here until his death in 1923; the same year Louise moved in with her daughter Mrs. Charles Lamphere.

James Armstrong
Photograph from the
Clare Sentinel 1923

Olevin and Cora Breen purchased this house in 1925, after they quit farming in Wise Township, Isabella County. He started life in 1885 in New York State and was married to Cora Fee, from Saint Louis, Missouri, in 1906. They settled east of Clare in 1915 and moved to this house eleven years later.

Charles Strange
Photograph from the
Clare Sentinel 1960

The Breens lived in the house until 1945, when it was sold to Charles Strange, who became a major figure in the development of the oil industry in Clare. Charles was born in Freestone, Texas in 1880, and came to Clare in 1929. Upon arriving in Clare, he set up an office on the first floor of the Doherty Hotel. In the 1930s he resided in the former Alfred Doherty house at 717 North McEwan Street. Charles Strange lived in this house until his death in 1960.

106 West Wheaton Avenue
Constructed in 1894

This house was constructed in 1894 by Lorenzo Goodman, but sadly, he only enjoyed it for one year. He passed away in 1895 at the age of twenty-six. He was raised in Birmingham, Michigan, and came to Clare in 1885 at the age of sixteen. For a short time he was employed at Cummer's Lumber Co. in Cadillac, but most of his adult life was spent working in the hardware store of his father, William H. Goodman. He married Bertha Feighner in 1893, and they had one son who passed away at four months of age. Bertha lived here until 1900 when she left for South Bend, Indiana, to work for her brother-in-law, Frank Goodman, in his insurance office.

After Bertha Goodman left for Indiana, John Wilson and then W. P. Enders both rented this house. John Wilson was the Wilson of the Wilson & Sutherland clothing business, located at the southwest corner of Fourth and McEwan Streets.

In 1903 George and Katherine McKeever purchased this house and lived here until 1923. George was the previous owner of the houses at both 210 and 303 East State Street. George continued to work at his shingle mill business in the early 1900s. In 1905 he formed a partnership with James Tatman. The agreement stated that both had a half interest in each other's grocery store and shingle mill businesses. After this partnership was dissolved in 1913, George McKeever once again assumed sole ownership of his shingle mill business. In addition, in 1913, George opened his own grocery store in his building located at the corner of Sixth and McEwan Streets.

George lived in this house until 1918 when he moved into the second floor of his building at Sixth and McEwan Streets. He rented this house to a Mr. Wilkinson at the time. The following year the McKeevers moved to the Detroit area, but the house was not sold until 1931.

The first half of the 1930s has several changes of ownership for this house. A June 1931 *Clare Sentinel* article reports William E. Bowler as purchasing this house. Another article, one year later, talks of Mr. and Mrs. E. A. Troop as "becoming the owners of the Bowler property...known to many as the McKeever home." One more article, from March 1934 writes, "Mr. and Mrs. E. A. Throop are moving from the O'Connor residence known to many as the McKeever house...W. E. Bowler and family expect to occupy this residence in the future."

The main owners of this house from the 1930s to the 1950s were William and Jennie Bowler. William Bowler was born in Ishpeming, Michigan, in 1881, and came to the Clare area at about the age of five. In his early adult life, he owned and operated farms in Grant Township and also worked as a rural mail carrier. He married Jennie Bates from Clare County in 1905. Mr. Bowler was employed with the Clare County Road Commission for several years and was at one point its chairman. He also served as the Superintendent of County Highways within the Michigan State Highway Department. In 1932 William Bowler opened the Twin Elms Golf Course four miles north of Clare. By the 1950s this golf course was known as the Clare Country Club. William Bowler lived in this house until his death in 1956, Jennie survived until 1982.

William's son, William "Eddie" Bowler Jr., had the misfortune of losing his life in World War II.

William "Eddie" Bowler
Photograph from the
Forrest Meek Collection

Eddie was a graduate of Clare High School, Central Michigan College of Education, and was one semester from graduating from the Detroit College of Law before he enlisted in the Navy Air Corp in February 1942. He received his flight training at both the Naval Reserve Aviation Base in New Orleans, Louisiana, and the Naval Air Station at Pensacola, Florida. He was commissioned an Ensign in October 1942. He married Pauline McDowell while in Seattle, Washington, in June 1943. He died at the age of twenty-six when his plane was lost somewhere in the South Pacific on August 14, 1943.

William and Jennie's daughter Lucetta married Lieutenant Alfred Austin in 1944. Alfred graduated high school in Bellaire, Michigan. Both Alfred and Lucetta attended the Central Michigan College of Education. Alfred enlisted in the Navy Air Corp in 1940 and after Pearl Harbor was stationed on the aircraft carrier Marcus Island. He fought in the battles of Leyte, Luzon, parts of the Philippines, Palau, and the South China Sea. He was honored by receiving the Distinguished Flying Cross in 1945. By 1948 he had achieved the rank of Lieutenant Commander and was reporting to

Alfred Austin
Receiving His Distinguished Flying Cross
Photograph from the
Forrest Meek Collection

the Grosse Ile Naval Air Station while at the same time attending dental school at the University of Detroit. He graduated from dental school in 1950 and set up an office in the J. E. Doherty block. Alfred and Lucetta lived in the apartment of this house upon their arrival to Clare and lived here into the 1970s.

314 East Second Street
Constructed in 1895

George Lee was a veteran of the Civil War, serving in Company E of the 65th Ohio. He came to Clare in 1874 and became a successful businessman. His wood frame store, where he sold grain, feed, hay, bricks, etc., was located in the middle of the east side of the 400 Block of North McEwan. He also owned large warehouses on both sides of the Pere Marquette railroad tracks to the south of his store. In 1895, after twenty-one years of business in Clare, George Lee built this house on the end of East Second Street. The newspaper reported that its location on the top of the hill made it "quite conspicuous".

In 1907 Lee purchased the Star Theatre which was housed in the newly constructed building at 120 West Fourth Street. The following year he moved the theatre to the Dunwoodie Building on the northwest corner of Fifth and McEwan.

Although he remained in Clare, Lee sold his house to the sixty-one-year-old Daniel Lamont in 1908. Mr. Lamont was born in Pickerin, Ontario, in 1847, and he married Isabella Shedden in 1874. They remained in Ontario until 1880 when they moved to Rosebush. He worked there as a carpenter until 1897 when he was appointed the village Post Master.

Prior to the death of Daniel Lamont in 1920, the house was occupied for a short time by Frank Wahl; in 1921 it was sold to Charles Heiser, who had recently quit farming near Arthur Center in Clare County.

Just like Daniel Lamont, Charles Heiser was in his sixties when he first occupied this house. He was born in Harrisburg, Pennsylvania in 1861. When he was four years old his family moved to Spencerville, Ohio. His father was a soldier fighting in the Civil War when the family moved, and he joined them later. While in Spencerville he met and married Della Parrott, but their marriage only lasted seven-and-a-half months when she died in 1884. One year later he married Mary Jane Slentz of Monticello, Ohio. In 1903 Charles and Mary moved to Arthur Township, where they purchased and cleared an 80-acre plot of land. They moved to Clare in 1921 when they purchased this house. Charles passed away in 1941. After Charles death, Mary Heiser moved in with her son Warren Heiser who lived at 108 Pearl Street, Vernon City. Mary passed away in July 1962 at the age of ninety-eight.

203 East Fifth Street
Constructed in 1903

Perry Brown was a pioneer farmer in Shiawassee County, Michigan. He was born in Venice Township in 1848 and married Elisabeth Fields in 1871.

Elisabeth was born in 1851 in New York City and came to Shiawassee County with her parents in 1856. Perry moved to the Clare area sometime in the late 1880s. Perry ran a large sheep farm west of Clare. In 1903 Perry moved to Clare and built this house.

Elisabeth passed away in 1912, and two years later he married Agnes Martin, a childhood friend. Agnes Martin was born Agnes Lyttle in 1854 and was also a native of Shiawassee County. Agnes married Harvey Martin, who passed away 1902. Agnes died in 1919, and Perry married a third time in 1920. This time it was to the forty-two-year-old native of Vernon Township, Eva Seeley. Perry Brown died in 1927, and Eva retained ownership of the house, but moved back to her parent's farm in Vernon Township. It appears she had no further connection with this house until it was sold in 1942.

Even before Perry Brown's death, the house was being rented as an office and apartments. In both 1923 and 1924, R. E. Goslow a chiropractic doctor from Mount Pleasant was advertising this house as his office. In 1927 Andrew Friz began renting one of the apartments here for his family. Andrew was the owner and manager of Friz Undertaking. Friz Undertaking purchased Gould Undertaking in 1921, and the business was located in the north unit of the Dunwoodie Building at 605 North McEwan. It seems Andrew Friz only lived here for about one year.

Andrew Friz
Photograph from the
Clare Sentinel 1921

Eva Brown's brother, Fred Seeley, located his insurance office in this building from 1936 to 1938. He was also very active in that time period in advertising the apartment units in the house for rent. A Mrs. Clark was renting here in 1936, and Mr. and Mrs. Harold MacAlonan were renting in 1939. Eva's sister, Edna Seeley, likewise advertised the availability of rental units in the house from 1940 to 1941.

The house was sold to Douglas and Minnie Smith in 1942. Douglas was born in Detroit in 1900. He was a veteran of World War I, serving in the 721st Co. Motor Transport Corps. He was discharged in 1919. The following year, he came to Clare with his parents. In 1921 he married Minnie Verrette, a native of Vernon Township. In the late 1920s, he was doing vulcanizing and battery work at James Clute's garage. By the mid-1930s he was employed as an electrician in the Ford factory in Detroit. He returned to Clare about 1940 and purchased this house in 1942. He passed away in September of that same year.

Minnie Smith continued to live in the house after Douglas' death and even operated her Min-ette Beauty Shop from the house. She married Ferdinand Seibt in 1945. He was a native of Coleman who was born in 1916. They called this house their home after their wedding. The newlywed couple Richard and Kathleen Paxton rented the upstairs apartment in 1952.

For an unknown period of time in the 1950s Ferdinand's mother, Rosella Seibt, was living with her son's family. Rosella was a native of Tamas Rackus, Austria-Hungary. She was born in 1878 and immigrated to Cleveland, Ohio, in 1907. She came to Michigan in 1911, and her husband of twenty-four years passed away in 1921. Rosella departed this life in 1956 while residing here.

Minnie and Ferdinand sold the house in 1958 to Charles Fortlander.

307 East Sixth Street
Constructed in 1904

Loretta Jane Callam, also known as Jennie, was one of the earliest settlers of the Village of Clare. She was the youngest of seven children born to Peter and Christine Callam. Jennie was born in Ontario, Canada, in 1863, and came to Clare on the first passenger train to stop here on November 20, 1870. Her father, Peter Callam, arrived in Clare earlier that year, working for William McEwan to survey the original plat of the Village of Clare. In 1871 he opened the first grocery store in this town, and also became the first post master.

In 1880 Archie Gordanier came to Clare, and two years later married Jennie Callam. While in Clare, Archie had a number jobs. For several years he worked in the grocery business, for a time he worked as a barber at the Calkins Hotel, later he worked in the lumber business, and finally was in charge of the oil delivery, to Clare, for the Standard Oil Company.

Jennie Gordanier eventually obtained a job as a teacher in the Clare public school. A 1884 *Clare County Press* article reports Dennis Alward was serving as the school principal and earning a salary of $60.00. Alfred J. Doherty was the Intermediate class teacher, earning a salary of $40.00. Jennie taught the Primary class and made a salary of $30.00.

In August of 1903, Jennie's husband Archie passed away as a result of tuberculosis. The following year Jennie purchased this property on Sixth Street and had this house constructed.

After Archie's death, Jennie took over her former husband's position with the Standard Oil Company. However, by 1911 she began working in the ticket office of the Ann Arbor Railroad. It was there that she met her second husband Leonard McCulloch.

Leonard was born in Grand Rapids in 1863. He lived for a time in Ludington, but eventually obtained a job at the Ann Arbor Railroad depot in Farwell. He became the Station Agent (person in charge of the depot) there in 1893, and later became the first Station Agent at Rosebush. His work at the Rosebush depot required him to daily travel to and from Clare. It was during these trips that Leonard met Jennie, and they were married in 1913.

Instead of moving to Rosebush, it was decided that Leonard would move into Jennie's house in Clare. He made the trip to work at the Rosebush depot on a daily basis until he retired in 1937. Ten years later Leonard died of a heart ailment.

Jennie McCulloch lived another ten years. The last nine years of her life were spent at a convalescent home in Morley. Jennie passed away in 1957 at the age of ninety-three.

313 East Seventh Street
Constructed in 1904

For a good portion of this house's history, it has been a rental property. It was constructed in 1904 by Dr. Thomas Maynard for that purpose.

Thomas Maynard was born in 1841 in the state of Ohio. His parents later took the family by covered wagon to Indiana and then Illinois. He started to study medicine at the age of nineteen, working during the day and studying at night. He graduated in 1866 from a college in Columbia City, Indiana. He then moved to the Clare area where he purchased land in section ten of Vernon Township. In his obituary, the *Clare Sentinel* did an excellent job of recounting the conditions of his early life when he first arrived in Vernon Township:

...At the time there were only about forty settlers in the entire township and the only roads were trails that were impassable for a double team of horses.

Clare did not exist as a town at that time and the young doctor did not own a horse or have money enough to either purchase or hire one, so he went on foot to make sick calls. He traveled twenty-five hundred miles the first year he lived in Vernon Township.

Quoting from some of the reminiscences of those early days that he had written a few years ago,

Dr. Thomas Maynard
Photograph from the Forrest Meek Collection

"The people were kind to me, we were all in common with each other, and all of us had good appetites and not much money and our credit was little below par. Our nearest trading point was Mt. Pleasant and the road was not passable except for a pony. I came over the road with a pony whose weight was under eight hundred pounds and he carried two hundred pounds of flour, sixty pounds of fresh pork, and twenty pounds of groceries, and to dedicate the load, I also rode the pony, making four hundred and twenty pounds that he carried."

A few years later, he purchased a pony and made his long trips on horseback, and although he was obliged to take his compensation in meat, vegetables, and articles which the Indians had manufactured, or perhaps receive nothing at all, this pioneer physician continued to minister unto all who called for his professional services. During an epidemic of smallpox, he continued in the saddle for the greater part of twenty-seven days.

Dr. Maynard did not have an easy life by any stretch of the imagination. He married Josephine Berry in 1871. They had four children, but only his son Albert lived to adulthood. Josephine also died in 1891. Thomas married Idella Westmiller in 1893. They had two children that both died in infancy. Idella passed away in June 1916 and his son Albert died two months later. Thomas Maynard married a third time in 1918 to Elizabeth Koontz, and she passed away in 1926.

When Dr. Maynard built this house he also built the one immediately to the east at 315 East Seventh. He sold the house at 315 East Seventh to Charles Clifton in 1919, but retained ownership of this house until his death in 1929. At the time of his death, he only had two remaining heirs. His son Albert had two sons, Perry and Thomas Maynard Jr., who inherited the house. Both were lawyers living in Detroit. Thomas immediately sold his interest in the house to Perry.

Perry Maynard lost the house to foreclosure in the 1930s. It was purchased by Alice Beemer and Cordelia Smalley in 1935. They sold it to Joseph and Sarah Hendrie in 1943. Joseph Hendrie retained ownership of the house and used it as a rental property until his death in 1959.

Some the people who have rented this house prior to

Sarah and Joseph Hendrie
Photograph from the
Clare Sentinel 1937

the 1960s include M. J. Brown 1910s, Melvin E. Green 1920s, Mr. and Mrs. Arthur Fleming 1930s, Helen Griffen early 1940s, Mr. and Mrs. Carl Lear mid-1940s, Pearl McKenzie early 1950s, and Neil Sowle late 1950s.

Pearl McKenzie
Photograph from the
Forrest Meek Collection

Of these Pearl McKenzie is of particular interest. She came from Reed City in 1938 to take over the management of Robert Gardner's gas station at the west end of Clare on the north side on US-10. With the change in management, the station became the Modern Maid gas station. The station was staffed entirely by female attendants, who wore blue, wine, or brown overalls and blouses. Although a relatively new idea when it came to Clare, the Modern Maid concept had already received favorable state-wide attention. It is unknown how long the Modern Maid gas station operated in Clare. The last mention of it in the newspaper is in 1942.

604 Pine Street
Constructed in 1904

1904 was one of the major years for construction in the City of Clare. Sixteen houses were built, and thirteen commercial buildings. In addition, many houses had additions built, and stone foundations or cellars added. Poplar trees were removed, other trees planted, and cement sidewalks built. This house is one of the five houses in this book that was constructed in that year.

Hugh Neelands was born in Brampton, Ontario, in 1881. He attended schools in Canada before graduating in 1901 from the Dental Department of the University of Michigan. He came to Clare the next year and set up his dental practice in the Doherty-Duncan Block above Leusenkamp Brothers store. He eventually moved his office to the second floor of the Elden Block.

Hugh and Jennie Neeland
Photograph from the
Clare Sentinel 1903

In 1902, he married Jennie Sexsmith, a native of Clare. They built this house in 1904 and remained here until 1910 when they moved to Metaline Falls, Washington.

Elmer and Josephine Anderson purchased the house four years after the Neelands moved out of Clare. Elmer originated from Wexford County Michigan and was born in 1882. He attended Ferris Institute and graduated as a pharmacist in 1901. He first obtained a job in Newberry and then in Cadillac before coming to Clare in 1905. When arriving in Clare he purchased The City Drug Store from Charles L. Pickle. It was located in the building at 520 North McEwan. When A. J. Doherty finished the construction of his brick block building next door at 518 North McEwan in 1911, Elmer Anderson's drug store was the first business to lease the property. In fact, the Anderson Drug Store operated in the same location in downtown Clare from 1911 to the early 1980s. He converted it to a Rexall Drug Store in the early 1920s.

Elmer married Josephine Green in 1906. She was born in Central Lake in 1884. She moved to Cadillac and then to Clare in 1906. Elmer died while working at his store in January 1941. The house was deeded to the Anderson's three children in 1957, with Josephine holding a life lease on the property. Josephine passed away in 1964. She lived in this house exactly fifty years.

Elmer and Josephine Anderson
Photographs from the Clare Sentinel 1906

604 Pine Street
Circa 1904
Photograph from the Forrest Meek Collection

111

804 North McEwan Street
Constructed in 1904

By the time Alfred J. Doherty finished building this house in 1904, he had been a state senator for three years. Doherty served in the Michigan State Senate from 1901 to 1906 as the majority whip. As the majority whip, Doherty exerted a great deal of power and was given the derogatory term of "Bell Cow" by his opponents.

After his time in the Senate, Doherty was a member of the State Board of Agriculture from 1907 to 1913. He also served as the president of the State Public Domain Commission. From 1907 to 1919, he served as one the first statewide elected members of the Michigan State University Board of Trustees. He was appointed for several years as the Superintendent of the Michigan State Fair. In 1911 Doherty became the owner of the Municipal Water, Light, and Power Company of Mackinac Island. In addition to performing all these duties, he also served as a lobbyist for the Pullman Railroad Car Company.

In 1915, A. J. Doherty sold this house to his son-in-law and daughter William and Lyda Bicknell, but the Bicknells had been living here since 1912. A. J. Doherty moved across the street to his newly constructed house at 717 North McEwan.

William Bicknell was born in Clare in 1879. He worked for many years for his father, Nathan Bicknell, in the general merchandise business. He took over the operations of his father's business, the Bicknell Department Store, in

Alfred J. Doherty
*Photograph from the
Forrest Meek Collection*

William and Lyda Bicknell
Photographs from the Clare Sentinel 1902

1913, four years after his father's death. When the Citizens State Bank was organized in 1909, William Bicknell served as its director, a position he held until his death. Finally, Bicknell acted for several years as the director of the Doherty Motor Hotel Corporation.

In 1902 William Bicknell married Lyda Doherty. Lyda was the daughter of Alfred and Alice Doherty and was born in 1883. She graduated from Clare High School and later attended the Conservatory of Music at Albion College. Lyda passed away in 1946. William lived in this house for fifty-one years until his death in 1966.

From historic photographs, it can be seen that the roof has changed since the house was originally constructed. This was due to an electrical storm that set fire to the roof of the house in May 1916. The *Clare Sentinel* reported the incident as follows:

> The heavy storm of rain and hail on Sunday night was accompanied by a highly electric condition of the atmosphere. About 1:30 a.m. the fine residence of Wm. H. Bicknell was struck, the current splitting the big stone cap on the rear chimney, passing downward and firing the building in a bedroom, thence to the earth. The fire rapidly crept up and involved the whole roof and all above the third floor. The absence of the electric lights probably hampered the firemen somewhat in getting on the scene but after a comparatively brief time, they had the fire under control. It was indeed fortunate that rain was falling at the time or doubtless other buildings might have been fired. The sparks fell in showers on the roof of the John E. Doherty house next north of the burning building, but they were extinguished as soon as they fell.
>
> The work of the fire was largely confined to the roof. The damage below that is due to the water which of course deluged everything. Quite a quantity of furniture was taken out but more or less damaged. Everything above the third floor was burned, among

this being many books and ledgers belonging to A. J. Doherty that had never been removed...

A. J. Doherty's life is also discussed later in the book. His life is told in order by reading the histories of 806 and 808 North McEwan Streets, Kilarney Farm, 804 North McEwan Street, and then 717 North McEwan Street.

804 North McEwan Street
Circa 1911
Photograph from the Forrest Meek Collection

114 East State Street
Constructed in 1909

Between the time Edward A. White sold his house at 308 East Fifth Street in 1890 and built this house in 1909, a lot happened in his life. In early 1890 Edward moved back to West Bay City to manage the jewelry store of his former boss, Stephen Swart. He returned the following year and built a house on State Street, and located his jewelry business in the Opera House building, and later that year in the Wolskey building. He left again in 1900 to work for one year repairing and adjusting high-grade railroad watches in Indianapolis. He sold his jewelry business in 1905 to M. D. Ellis, while he pursued his farming interests in West Grant Township. The following year he moved to Jackson, but a few months later was back in Clare. On his return, he repurchased the jewelry business of M. D. Ellis. After the downtown fire of 1907, Mr. White along with Edgar Welch and Phillip Bennett built the building at 114 West

Fourth Street. Edward White occupied the southwest quarter of the building for his jewelry store, while the rest of the building served the Clare Sentinel newspaper and print shop.

In 1913 Ed White took on his son Carl as a partner in the jewelry business. The business was sold in 1916 to Cyrus Mummon. White sold this house in 1918 to William McAllister and moved to Saginaw the following year. He eventually made his residence in New Smyrna, Florida. He was able to sell his storefront on West Fourth Street in 1912 before he moved, but the 511 North McEwan Street building was not sold until 1925.

The second owner of this house, William McAllister, was the manager of the Clare Hay, Grain, and Bean Co. when he purchased this house. The Clare Hay, Grain, and Bean Co. later changed its name to the Clare Elevator Company. In 1921 McAllister, in partnership with George Johnson, purchased the Clare Elevator Company. Mr. McAllister sold his interest in the Clare Elevator Company in April 1923, and by June of that same year had purchased the furniture stock of D. E. Mater and located his new business, McAllister Dependable Furniture, in the "Rhoades Block" at 523 North McEwan. McAllister operated his store until 1929 when he was bought out by the Clare Hardware and Furniture Company. By 1930 he was selling insurance out of his house. In November of 1931, he sold his house and moved to Plymouth where he accepted a position in the engineering department for the State of Michigan.

Charles and Olive Weidner purchased the house from William McAllister in 1931. The Weidners were from Harrison and it does not appear that they ever lived here. The *Clare Sentinel* mentions Florence White Gay living here in 1940, and a Mrs. Gardner in 1946.

Lewis Siegel purchased this house in 1949. He had been the owner of Northland Hardware, at 412 North McEwan, since 1946. Mr. Siegel served in the U. S. Field Artillery during World War II and became acquainted with Clare as a result of owning a cabin at Budd Lake in Harrison. Siegel sold his business in 1952 but retained ownership of the building at 412 North McEwan until 1973. Prior to moving his family to Jackson, South Carolina, in 1952, he sold his house to Dr. H. Gordon Henry.

Dr. Henry came to Clare in 1951 to take charge of the surgery department after the Clare Hospital was purchased by new owners and renamed the Clare General Hospital (Osteopathic). Dr. Henry stayed in Clare for only a couple years. He along with a group of doctors purchased a sixteen-bed hospital in Au Gres, Michigan. He sold this house to Jerome and Gladys Flood in 1953.

214 East State Street
Constructed in 1916

Daniel Mater was born in 1864 in the town of Fulton, Ohio. When he was seven years old he moved with his family to Nashville, Michigan. His wife Sarah was born in 1867 in Nashville, Michigan, and they were wed in 1888. The day after their wedding they began the journey that took them to Clare. Upon arriving in Clare, they built a house on East Seventh Street. Daniel Mater spent his early days in Clare working as a carpenter. Daniel and his brother George formed a partnership (Mater Brothers) and constructed their own mill where they manufactured custom trim for the construction and remodeling work they did on Clare buildings. In the mid-1890s, Daniel moved his family out of the city and relocated on a farm northeast of Clare on Dover Rd. He returned to Clare in 1916 and constructed this house.

119

Daniel Mater
Photograph from the
Forrest Meek Collection

Three years after returning to Clare, Daniel purchased the furniture business of Harrold Brothers, and relocated it to the north part of the Tatman Building. Mater confessed that he had no retail experience, but he did know how to make quality furniture. The business was successful and eventually moved to 115 East Fourth Street. In 1922 Daniel Mater constructed the house at 313 East Sixth Street, and moved there the same year. He sold the 214 East State Street house in 1924 to Benjamin and Victoria Mercer.

Ben Mercer was born in Belfast, Ireland, in 1871. He immigrated to Canada at the age of ten and moved to Saginaw in 1896. While in Canada he met Victoria Hazelwood, and they were married in 1889. Victoria was born in 1871 in Raglan, Ontario.

While in Saginaw, Benjamin Mercer worked as a representative of the Champion Machine Company and at a different time the Gale Manufacturing Company. He was a popular Saginaw citizen and served as mayor of the city from 1919 to 1922. His term in office was noted for the substituting of streetcar service in the city with public bus service. He moved his family to Clare in 1922 and purchased this house for his place of residence.

In 1923 Ben Mercer purchased from William Webb his interest in the Clare Hardware and Implement Company. He joined Mortimer Gallagher in the operation of the business until they sold the store to Stanley Burdo in 1936. In 1936 Mercer partnered with a group of Clare businessmen and founded the Clare Travel Coach

Company with Ben acting as the company's secretary. The company was short lived as it was out of business by the 1940s.

Benjamin Mercer passed away in late 1940, and his wife Victoria moved with her daughter Victoria to Miami, Florida, and then New York City. She sold the house in 1940.

Harold and Genevieve Fleming purchased this house after the death of Benjamin Mercer. Harold was born in 1901 and Genevieve in 1900. They were married in Ithaca in 1925 and moved to Clare from Chicago in 1932. Harold opened the new HI-Speed gas station on the southeast corner of Seventh and McEwan Streets in 1937. He retained ownership of it until 1950 when he sold it to Leonard and Leon Stanley. In addition to

Benjamin Mercer
Photograph from the
Clare Sentinel 1925

selling gasoline and other automotive supplies, Harold opened a sporting goods store in this location. He was also a dealer of REO Speedwagon Automotives. The Flemings lived in this house until the mid-1950s.

216 East Seventh Street
Constructed in 1917

At sixty-seven years of age, Harvey Fairman had already lived a long hard life of farming before he built this house in 1917. He originated from Thurlow, Ontario, and married Emily Hart from Tyendinaga, Hastings County, Ontario in 1873. Six years later they arrived in Leaton, Michigan, before they purchased a farm in Wise Township. Harvey's health was deteriorating to such a point that in 1902 they gave up farming and moved to Clare.

In 1913, Emily suffered a stroke which she never fully recovered from. Harvey only enjoyed his new house for two years due to his death in 1919. After his death, his wife Emily moved out and entered into the care of her son Lewis. Emily survived three more years before passing away in 1922.

Lewis Fairman arranged the sale of this house to his cousin James Glass in 1920. James came from Tyendinaga, Ontario and was born in 1872. In 1893 he came to live with his aunt and uncle, Harvey and Emily Fairman, on their farm in Wise Township. The next fall he moved to Farwell for six years were he stayed with J. Gardiner. After spending an undetermined amount of time "railroading" in the west, James returned to his uncle in Herrick and lived there for three years. He eventually came to Clare, where he worked at the Lloyd livery.

He married Carrie McClelland in 1905, who came to Clare from Saginaw. After their marriage, the couple moved to Dover where they opened a mercantile store. Due to James' poor health, he passed away in 1922. His wife and children left Dover and moved into this house until 1924. When Carrie returned to Clare she obtained a job with the William H. Bicknell and Company Store. She continued her employment there until 1934 when she was hospitalized at the Harper Hospital in Detroit. She recovered but passed away the following year.

Her son James Russell Glass and his wife Margaret inherited the house after his mother's death but used it as a rental property. Mr. and Mrs. Nelson Bernier were renting the property prior to July 1940. An advertisement in a September 1947 issue of the *Clare Sentinel* noted "Chris the Tailor" as using the house for a business. James Russell Glass owned the house until 1950 when he sold it to John and Blanche Stoll who also used it for an investment property.

304 East Sixth Street
Constructed in 1919

Norris Elden was born in 1888 to William and Mary Elden. He spent his early life in Clare working for his father in his bazaar store business. He left for Chicago in 1906 and was hired at the Marshall Field and Company Store. He married Adelaide Arnold in 1909. She was born in Mount Pleasant in 1886 and attended the Mount Pleasant Normal School. She came to Clare and taught fourth grade. It is unknown how Norris and Adelaide met, since he was in living in Chicago.

For several years after their marriage, Norris and Adelaide moved a great deal, with Norris changing jobs frequently. The year after they were married Norris accepted a position at Doughty's dry goods store in Mount Pleasant. By 1911 the family was living in Evart and in 1912 they were back in Clare. When he arrived back in Clare Norris began working at the Wilson-Davy Company Store.

This also proved to be a short term job, because Elden stopped work there in 1914 to work the family farm north of town. Farming lasted only two years and Norris took a job in 1916 working at the Bicknell Store in Clare.

This house at 304 East Sixth Street was constructed in 1919 on the lot immediately behind the house that Norris's parents had lived in since 1889. Almost at the same time, Norris's employment seemed to stabilize. In 1920 Thomas Holbrook, who occupied William Elden's business block on McEwan Street, was relocating to a different building. Norris Elden along with Fred Thompson and Simon Bogardus opened a men's and boy's clothing store in that location. This partnership lasted until 1924 when the Wilson-Davy Company purchased the entire stock of the Thompson Elden Bogardus store. With the buyout, Elden became a stockholder, treasurer, and manager of the store. Adelaide was also employed at the store and served as a department head and merchandise buyer for thirty years.

Norris's son Neal Elden was stationed for a time in England during World War II. While there he married June Carmen in February 1944. The following year she came to Clare to live with Norris and Adelaide. The January 19, 1945, issue of the *Clare Sentinel* recounts her life in England and journey to the United States:

> Mrs. Elden has had many thrilling and grueling experiences in war torn England, as well as on the Continent. The building in which she was employed in London was bombed three times and she spent as much as fourteen days at a time in the seclusion of the private shelter at their home, with members of the family and their pet dog and cat.
>
> Although she encountered unusually heavy snow in Canada, Mrs. Elden was deeply impressed by the comparative peace and tranquility of Canada and the United States and likes Clare very much.
>
> Only people who have actually seen the devastation and endured the mental agony of war can

imagine her appreciation of a community free from the fear of bombings and other horrors of war.

Norris retired from business life when the Davy store was sold in 1963. Besides his retail business life in Clare, Norris was also an accomplished musician and vocalist. He sang and led many church and community musical events. He passed away in 1968 at the age of seventy-nine and was followed in death the next year by his wife Adelaide at the age of eighty-three. They had both lived in this house since the time it was constructed in 1919.

701 Beech Street
Constructed in 1921

William Francis Clute was born in 1881 on a farm in Sheridan Township. When he turned eighteen he was hired in the VanBrunt bakery. He worked at the bakery in the winter months, and returned to his family farm in the spring. In 1901 he began his medical studies at the Saginaw Medical College. After two years of study in Saginaw, he attended the Detroit College of Medicine, where he graduated with his medical degree in January 1905.

In June of the same year, he moved to Gladwin where he set up his first Physician and Surgeon office. After practicing in Gladwin for an unknown period of time, Dr. Clute received an urgent request from Dr. R. A. Gray to come to Clare and practice medicine with his son, Frank R. Gray. Dr. R. A. Gray was familiar with William Clute since his childhood and thought he would be a suitable partner for his son. Dr. Clute came to Clare, and along with

Dr. Frank Gray set up an office on the second floor of the Citizens Bank building. The two men practiced until about 1914 when Dr. Gray headed out to the northwest and Dr. Clute purchased a building on North McEwan Street for his office. His building would one day be the office of Dr. Kuno Hammerberg.

Dr. Clute built this house in 1921. He married the twenty-one-year-old local women, Delia Harrington in 1930. They had one child, and then, in 1934, Dr. William Clute passed away. After his death, Delia and their daughter Frances Gayle left Clare so Delia could obtain an education in the medical field.

Dr. William Clute
Photograph from the
Forrest Meek Collection

Donald Holbrook and Rev. Stanley Morrison were joint executors of William Clute's estate. Starting the year after his death they were advertising his house for rent. It is unknown who rented the house and for how long. In 1946 the two executors on behalf of Frances Gayle, who was still a minor, sold the house to James Olson.

James Olson had come to Clare with his wife Anna in 1933 and purchased the Ideal Theatre from John Asline. James was born in Manistee, Michigan in 1895 after his parents emigrated from Denmark. He served in World War I, and after the war purchased and managed a theater in Gaylord which he later sold. He married Anna Carlton while in Florida in 1921. Anna was born in New York City in 1899. After their marriage, they returned to Michigan and moved to East Jordan where James bought and sold another movie theater. He then moved to Detroit where he worked for the National Theater Supply Company. He resigned from there in 1933 and moved to Clare.

After purchasing the Ideal Theatre in Clare, James' brother George partnered with him in the theater business and purchased a film theater in Grayling. The two brothers later purchased two theaters in Houghton Lake, one in West Branch and one in Gaylord. Later, they added the Sundown Drive-in, one mile north of Rosebush, and another theater in Gaylord. George Olson died and left the management of the theater chain to his brother, James, who used Clare as his headquarters.

James Olson
*Photograph from the
Clare Sentinel 1944*

The Ideal Theater was the jewel of all his theaters. For a small town theater, it was among the first to have modern sound and reproduction equipment, along with air-conditioning and widescreen film showing.

James Olson was a friend of Walt Disney while James was managing a theater in Detroit in the 1920s. The story goes that Olson loaned Disney, who was badly in need of money, $1,500. "As a result, Clare always got to see and enjoy the Disney films on first-run dates at the same time as big city releases." This story was told by Hugh Maxwell in the *Clare Sentinel* in their January 19, 1967, issue.

James passed away in 1963. Since he also owned the house at 1601 North McEwan Street (the old Isaiah Leebove house) it is unknown which one he lived in. Anna Olson died in 1967, and the house was deeded to their daughter Gloria Olson, who owned the house until 1976.

211 East Sixth Street
Constructed in 1922

Norval Tibbils was born in 1891 in Shepherd, Michigan. He served in the Medical Corps of the 32nd Division of the U. S. Army during World War I. During the Battle of the Argonne his unit was gassed. Since that time he had a lung condition that he never fully recovered from. After the war, he attended and graduated from the Northern Illinois Optical College of Chicago. In 1919 he accepted a position in the optical room of the F. L. Klunzinger jewelry store in Mount Pleasant.

Norval Tibbils came to Clare in 1920 and purchased the entire stock of jewelry from Cyrus Hummon. Cyrus had purchased the stock of jewelry from White and Sons when they went out of business in 1916. All three jewelers had occupied the same location at 511 North McEwan, and the building had been used as a jewelry store continually since it was constructed in 1887.

Norval Tibbils
Photograph from the
Clare Sentinel 1940

Norval married Hilda Bogardus in 1922. Hilda was the daughter of Simon and Eva Bogardus of Clare and was born in 1896. They built this house the same year they were married.

In 1929 Simon Bogardus closed his grocery business at 513 North McEwan, and Norval moved his jewelry business there at the same time.

Norval was also active in the community in many different ways. He served as Commander of the Walter H. Larmon American Legion Post from 1921 to 1923. He was elected as the second ward alderman in 1934, 1935, 1939, and 1940. He was also elected mayor of the City of Clare in 1942. He never completed his term as mayor. He suffered a life ending heart attack while patronizing the Anderson Drug Store on a November evening in 1942.

Hilda continued to live in this house after Norval's death. She operated the jewelry store until selling it to Alice Loomis and Lena Irving for their Parkview Gift & Jewelry Shop. By the time Hilda had sold the jewelry business it was located on West Fifth Street. The old Bogardus grocery store building was being leased to the Consumers Power Company from about 1941. In 1945 Eva Bogardus, Hilda Tibbil's mother, deeded Hilda the building Consumers Power Company was leasing. Hilda owned that building until 1965. She lived at this house on East Sixth Street until her death in 1979.

1601 North McEwan Street
Wildwood Cabin Constructed in 1924
Leebove Addition Constructed from 1938 to 1939

The house located on this property is actually made up of two houses. The first log structure was constructed around 1924, the second more well-known addition was built in the late 1930s.

Walter and Alta Pettit built the log structure here as part of their sixteen acres "Wildwood Estate." Walter was born in 1883 and was the son of the noted local conservation officer Charles E. Pettit. He came to Clare at about the age of seventeen with his parents. Walter made a living in the building industry, and he exhibited his craftsmanship in the construction of this house. The May 5, 1932, *Clare Sentinel* wrote the following about his "Wildwood Estate;"

> Since purchasing the sixteen-acre estate eight years ago, Mr. and Mrs. Pettit have constantly improved the premises until the city now points with

pride to the "Wildwood". Many tourists have been attracted to it and were always welcomed by their host and hostess when they expressed their desire to wander about the natural growth of the timber and fish ponds, visit the overnight cabins, cross the rustic bridge over a small creek which leads to the Tobacco River, and climb the ladder to the "Sky Pilot" where one can enjoy the rustling of the breezes in the tree tops.

Mr. Pettit had his Wildwood Shop where he made rustic furniture and novelties, which was placed on sale during the summer season. The home was furnished throughout in rustic design, designed and made by Mr. Pettit and unusual workmanship on the buildings made exclusively by its owner made this an outstanding possession.

Wildwood Estate
Circa 1925
Photograph from the Forrest Meek Collection

Walter Pettit is also known for his 1924 gift to the City of Clare of what was then known as "Cedar Park." The park was located on the south side of the Tobacco River, just west of M-14, and contained eight and one-half acres. Pettit believed the park would be an excellent location for a fish hatchery, but the city converted the land to a recreation park. It was renamed "Pettit Park" in 1964.

Walter and Alta Pettit sold their "Wildwood Estate" to Isaiah and Enid Leebove in 1932. They purchased it with the plan of making it their summer home. Isaiah was born in 1895 in Pittsburg, Pennsylvania. He graduated with a law and finance degree in 1915 from Cumberland University in Lebanon, Tennessee. After college, he first moved to Texas where he was admitted to the Texas State Bar in 1916. By 1917 he had moved to Tulsa, Oklahoma, and was working as a lawyer specializing in oilfield leases. While in Tulsa, Leebove served as the in-house lawyer for the Livingston Oil Company and was also in partnership

Isaiah Leebove
On the Wildwood Estate
Photograph from the
Forrest Meek Collection

134

with the attorney Claude Rosenstein.

After serving five months in the army during the later part of 1918, he moved to New York and began connecting himself with members of New York's organized crime world. Two of his main contacts were Arnold Rothstein and Legs Diamond. He married Marcia Freedman, a daughter of the wealthy New York merchant Joseph Freedman in 1921. Isaiah worked as a lawyer for his father-in-law's Freedman Brothers Company business. In addition, Leebove was employed by the law firm Schiff, Sylvester and Harris. His most frequent clients were members of New York's underworld.

Leebove divorced his wife Marcia in 1924, and two years later married Enid Seaton. Enid was born in Jamaica but moved to Toronto with her widowed mother and siblings in 1911. She met Isaiah while she was working as a showgirl in New York.

Isaiah and Enid moved from New York to Detroit, Michigan in 1929. The real reasons behind this move are unknown. He most likely left New York because Arnold Rothstein, the man who was Leebove's main underworld connection, was murdered in 1928. Leebove had extended family members who lived in Detroit, he easily made connections with the Jewish organized crime group known as the "Purple Gang" when he arrived in Detroit, and oil had been discovered a few years earlier in the Central Michigan area that Leebove believed could be exploited for money laundering.

In early 1930 Leebove came to Clare representing the Mammoth Petroleum Company. The company originally operated out of the Doherty Hotel. In 1933 the company was reorganized into the Mammoth Producing and Refining Company. The reorganization was done in an attempt to disguise the previous company's illegal activities and to give more control of the company to members of the Purple Gang. In April 1937 the company moved to offices located on the second floor of the Citizens State Bank Building at 502 North McEwan Street. Later that same year the company moved into the building across the street that housed the former Clare County Savings Bank at 431 North McEwan.

Isaiah Leebove was a complicated man. Most people agreed that he was a pleasant and personable man. He did not hesitate to help someone in need. Yet on the same note, he cheated the local citizens of Clare out of thousands of dollars of investments. It was ultimately these types of dealings that cost him his life. On May 14, 1938, Jack Livingston, a business associate of Leebove's from as far back as his days in Tulsa, murdered Isaiah Leebove in the bar of the Doherty Hotel.

Just prior to his death Leebove had planned the addition to his house that can be seen from McEwan Street. Construction was only begun on it when he was killed. Although it seems Enid never lived in this house after her husband's death, tax records show that the construction of the house was finished while she was the owner.

James Ryan
Photograph from the
Robert Knapp Collection

By the end of 1939 the construction of the addition was completed and the following year Enid leased the house to James and Rachel Ryan. The Ryans purchased the house the following year.

James Ryan was a long time attorney from Mount Pleasant and ironically was on the defense team of Jack Livingston during his trial for the murder of Isaiah Leebove. At the time he purchased the house, James Ryan was the president of the Alma Trailer Company, which manufactured trailer homes in Alma, Michigan. The Ryans sold their home in 1956 to James and Anna Olson. James likely lived here until his death in 1963, and Anna passed away in 1967.

501 East Sixth Street
Constructed in 1936

Arthur Damoth was born in 1897 in Middleville, Michigan.His wife was born Velma Ross in 1895, and she was a native of Beaverton. The Damoths came to Clare from Grand Rapids in 1936. He purchased the Clare Realty Company from Eugene A. Throop when he arrived and changed the name to the Art Damoth Agency. He sold both real estate and insurance.

In October of 1936, three months after purchasing the realty business, he began the construction of this house. The Damoths lived here until 1941 when they

Arthur Damoth
Photograph from the
Clare Sentinel 1944

137

constructed a new log and fieldstone residence on the north bank of the Tobacco River.

This house, on Sixth Street, was sold to John and Bernice Battle in 1941. The Battles were from Mount Pleasant, and John was the owner of John Battle Motor Sales in Mount Pleasant. He had been operating the business since around 1926. The Battles owned the house for about two years when they sold to Sam and Ruby Garfield in November 1943.

Sam Garfield was born in Detroit in 1902. He attended the Bishop Elementary School in Detroit. Some of the classes in the school were ungraded. These were a place for boys with troubled pasts when they could no longer be controlled by their parents. At the school, he became friends with Joey Bernstein and his brothers Izzy, Ray, and Abe. These boys started what became the infamous Purple Gang. The gang was known in Detroit for their illegal activities which included robbery, extortion, kidnapping, and bootlegging. By the late 1920s, they became the most powerful organized crime group in Detroit.

Garfield became acquainted with Isaiah Leebove in 1929 after Leebove moved to Michigan from New York. Garfield moved to Clare in 1930 and along with Leebove invested the illegally obtained Purple Gang money and laundered it in the booming Oil Industry of Central Michigan. From 1929 to 1932 Sam Garfield worked behind the scenes with Leebove and Leebove's Mammoth Petroleum Company. Garfield's job was to provide Leebove with the Purple Gang money needed to purchase the oil leases. When the Mammoth Petroleum Company was liquidated in 1933 and the Mammoth Producing and Refining Corporation was created, Garfield no longer worked behind the scenes, but was a member of the board of directors of the corporation.

After Leebove was murdered in 1938 Garfield became the president of the Mammoth Producing and Refining Corporation. In 1942 the business located to the newly constructed building at 515 North McEwan. They relocated again in 1961 to the second floor of the Citizens State Bank Building, at 502 North McEwan, after the bank moved to its new building north of Clare's downtown. At the same time Mammoth moved into the old bank building, Garfield

138

allowed the public library in Clare to use the building's first floor and basement. The library was renamed the Garfield Memorial Library in 1966 in honor of Sam Garfield's wife Ruby. Ruby lived in this house until her death in 1965. Sam Garfield called this house his home until he sold it in 1977 and moved to California.

208 & 210 East Seventh Street
Constructed in 1938

These two houses have occupied this lot since 1938. It cannot be confirmed but it appears that one was constructed during the summer of 1938, and the other was moved here from somewhere outside of Clare in October of the same year. The person responsible for them was a gentleman named Benton Loomis.

Mr. Loomis was sixty-two years old in 1938. He was born in Kent County, Michigan. in 1876. He was a longtime resident of Isabella County and Detroit before moving to Clare.

However, the interesting part of this property is what was located here before the two Benton Loomis houses. In 1887 the Free Methodist Society constructed a wood frame church on this lot. The church never purchased the property nor did William McEwan donate the property to the church. Prior to Benton Loomis owning the property, the Estate of William McEwan still owned this lot, and this had to have been one of the few remaining McEwan lots that were unsold. To complete the sale, McEwan's descendants from Seattle, Washington, New York, New York, London, England, Montreal, Canada, and Detroit and Bay City, Michigan, had to sign off on the sale.

The Free Methodist Church continued holding services here until December 1928. After that, the building was vacant for a number of years. It was finally purchased in 1935 by Clifford Lane, who tore it down and used the materials to build his house to the southeast of Clare.

Free Methodist Church
In right center of photograph,
looking east on Seventh Street,
Photograph from the Robert Knapp Collection

Part II
Lost
but not
Forgotten
Homes

Photograph from the Robert Knapp Collection

107 East Seventh Street
1884 to 1954

The Clare Methodist Episcopal Church on the north side of East Seventh Street's 100 block was constructed in 1878. It was a simple wood frame building with a gabled roof and small steeple. The M. E. Church was Clare's second church. The Congregational Church, Clare's first church, finished construction on their building in 1874. The Methodists went about six years without a parsonage. Starting in 1884 the construction of this house for the church parsonage was started and finished the following year.

A new stone and brick church building was constructed in the same location as the first wood frame building in 1910. The parsonage was repaired and updated throughout the years, but it was not replaced until 1954. With the church constructing a new parsonage it was decided to have this house removed from the site. Starting in the January 22, 1954, issue of the *Clare Sentinel*, the church was advertising the house for sale with the stipulation that it needed to be removed from the site by April 15th of the same year. It is unknown if someone purchased the house and moved it to another location, or if it was simply torn down.

For almost seventy years this house served as the residence for Clare's Methodists ministers and also the location of numerous weddings.

Photograph from the Forrest Meek Collection

111 West Fifth Street
1885 to 1928

The October 7, 1938, issue of the *Clare Sentinel* reported inaccurately that the W. S. Cooley house on West Fifth Street was the first brick house built in Clare. Wallace Cooley built this house in 1885, but the first brick house and, for that matter, the first brick building in Clare was constructed the year before by J. B. Husted.

Wallace Cooley was born in Wirt, New York in 1847. When he was seventeen years of age he was enlisted as a drummer boy in the 98th New York Infantry. His term of enlistment with the 98th was short, as he was then enrolled in the 85th. He was later discharged due to a severe illness.

He married Harriet Gleason on New Year's Day, 1869. She was born in 1841 and originated from Belfast, New York, the same hometown as A. J. Doherty. Wallace and Harriet moved to Midland in 1870 and Clare in 1871. When arriving in Clare he opened a harness shop, which he operated until 1880. Later that year he opened a livery across the street from the Congregational Church. He sold it to John Phinnesy in 1881. Starting in 1890 he owned and operated a marble and granite works.

Wallace Cooley was the first village treasurer and also held other minor offices for the village. He was appointed by Governor Aaron T. Bliss to be the County Agent for the Board of Corrections and Charities. Wallace was also an early newspaper publisher in Clare. In fact, he owned the first paper to be printed by steam power in the county.

Wallace lived in this house and worked at his monument business until his death in 1912. His wife lived in the house until she passed away in 1920. They had no children to deed the house to after their deaths.

A fire at the house in 1928 caused by a defective chimney was the ultimate demise of the house. Although the fire department acted quickly and confined the fire to the second floor, the house was not repairable and was torn down.

Photograph from the Robert Knapp Collection

806 North McEwan Street
1888 to 1971

This house and the one that was located to the north at 808 North McEwan Street were two of the unknown number of rental houses that A. J. Doherty built. Although he never lived here, just the fact that he built this house gives the opportunity to discuss his early life in Clare.

Alfred J. Doherty was born in 1858 and educated in the Genesee Seminary of Belfast, New York. His father was employed in the lumber business, specializing in the cutting and sale of timber for ship building. His father's work took him to various places around the Midwest, and he took his wife and son Alfred along. For a time the family resided in several different towns in Ohio.

Alfred Doherty married Alice Gleason in 1876 in Cuba, New York, and two years later moved to Clare with their infant son, Floyd. After living in Clare for a few months they purchased the house at 611 North McEwan. One of their other sons, Frank, was born at that house. They lived at 611 North McEwan until 1883 when they constructed a dwelling adjoining Dennis Alward's property.

Doherty's first job in Clare was a fireman in one of the village's shingle and lumber mills. The first known mention of Doherty in the newspaper is in 1878 when he spotted a fire in the rear of a wing of the Nicolls House Hotel. By December 1879 A. J. Doherty was employed at Trevidick's drug store. The following year he changed jobs and was working in the clothing business in Wolskey's store.

He taught school starting in 1881 and stopped when he opened his hardware store in 1885. He started as a teacher in the Crawford settlement, then moved to the Dover School, and finished in the Clare school. He continued to work while teaching to generate extra income. In his first summer off after teaching in the Crawford school, he went back to work in Trevidick's drug store. In 1883 he became an insurance agent and located his office at Trevidick's Store. His was the first insurance business in the area and covered Clare, Isabella, and Midland counties.

The Doherty Hardware Store opened in 1885 just south of the southeast corner of McEwan and Fifth Streets. In 1887 he relocated that business to a newly erected brick block he constructed on the southeast corner of the above-mentioned intersection. Four years later he constructed an Opera House building on the lot south of his hardware business. Doherty also built a two-story six-storefront brick building on the west side of the 400 block of North McEwan in 1900, and a two-story brick commercial building at 518 North McEwan in 1911.

He was also awarded the contract for the construction of the school house in district No. 2 of Hatton and Arthur. One additional building some people might feel is of note is an ice house he constructed for the Grasser & Brand Brewing Company of Toledo, Ohio. The ice house was located north of the freight depot in Clare along the Ann Arbor & North Michigan railroad. It was able to hold about two car loads of ice and 300 kegs of beer. The ice house was to be the company's distribution point for Northern Michigan.

A. J. was also a major developer of utilities for the village of Clare. In 1886 Doherty connected his house and store "telephonically." He later connected other buildings within Clare by phone. In 1897 he strung a phone line between Clare and Mount Pleasant which connected Clare with the state line. From 1898 to 1899 he extended the phone line from Midland to Clare, and then past Clare to Farwell and Harrison. The Bell Telephone Office was located in the Doherty Hardware building.

The Doherty Electric Light Co. was powered by a dam on the Tobacco River in 1891. At first, it only supplied power for Doherty's Hardware Store and a few surrounding buildings. In 1894 Doherty along with other investors had created the Clare Electric Co. which supplied power to the rest of the city. The power plant was located south of the railroad tracks just to the east of McEwan Street. By July 1895 there were seven-and-a-half miles of electric wire strung in the city.

Water is the final utility which Doherty controlled. Along with C. H. Clark, Doherty purchased the city water-works in 1895. The plant was located immediately to the east of the Clare Electric Company. Doherty improved it and in 1906 he relocated it to the Clare City Park bordering Fifth, Fourth and Beech Streets.

Doherty was also directly involved in the Clare Wooden Ware Company and was an investor in the Clare Furnace Company.

Alfred Doherty's son, Floyd, acquired this house in 1902. As mentioned earlier, Floyd came to Clare as an infant in 1878. After graduating from the Clare school he attended Olivet College. Starting in November 1893 Floyd was the local representative for Witter's Steam Laundry headquartered in Saginaw. By 1896 he was employed with the Evart Electric Light Company. In 1897 he partnered with his father and brother Frank in the Doherty & Sons Hardware business. Floyd must not have been an active partner in the business because at the turn of the century he was working in Kalamazoo for the Michigan Bell Telephone Company. Alfred Doherty turned the hardware business over to his sons in 1903, and the following year Floyd sold his business interest to Frank. Floyd returned to the steam laundry business in 1902 when he purchased the Pearl Steam Laundry from Mr. Rukenbrod, and renamed it the Monarch. He owned the laundry for a short three months before he sold it to R. A. Rapson. Floyd was, for a long time, the manager of the Doherty Opera House. He was also famous for being the first person in Clare to own an automobile.

Floyd Doherty
Photograph from the
Clare Sentinel 1903

Floyd Doherty married Josephine Storey in December 1901. Josephine originated from Genesee County but moved to Clare in 1899 to live with her sister. Floyd and Josephine lived in this house until 1904, when they moved to Lansing. Floyd rented the house to W. H. Van Horn in 1905.

John Doherty purchased the house from Floyd in 1906 and moved in the following year. John was a brother of Alfred Doherty, but he was closer in age to his nephew Floyd. Alfred was fifteen years older than John, and John was seven years older than Floyd. John and Floyd appeared to be good friends. The newspaper reported that Floyd Doherty was the groomsman for John's wedding.

John was born in 1871 in Belfast, New York. He moved to Coleman, Michigan, in 1892 and went into the hardware, undertaking and furniture business with his brother Joseph. He married Nina Spring in 1896, and she passed away along with her new born baby in 1898. He married Helen Coots in 1900. Helen was born in Angelica, New York, in 1875. The couple moved to Clare in 1902 where he continued in the undertaking and furniture business. He later sold the furniture portion of the business and added plumbing and heating. It is unknown where John operated his businesses out of, but it is possible he worked from his house. He first lived in a house on State Street before purchasing this house on

John Doherty
Photograph from the
Forrest Meek Collection

McEwan Street. When the Clare County Savings Bank moved out of their building at the southeast corner of Fifth and McEwan Streets in 1922, John moved his plumbing business in there. John co-owned that building with his brother, A. J., starting in the late 1920's. After A. J.'s death in 1929, John became the sole owner of the building.

John remodeled this house in 1934 and operate his funeral home from this location. Three years prior to this, the upstairs was divided into an apartment and was being advertised for rent.

John Doherty served several terms as Clare's city clerk, and also thirty years on the board for the Clare Chamber of Commerce. He retired from business around 1942 and passed away in 1952. His wife Helen continued to live in this house until her death in 1966, but she deeded the house to her son Michael in 1963. Helen's sister, Esther Wise, also lived in this house from 1936 until her passing in 1969.

John and Helen's son Michael was born in 1903. Michael graduated from the Haley Embalming School in Detroit. He married Hazel Parker in October 1925, and two months later moved to New York. They returned to Clare in 1927, when he joined his father in the plumbing and undertaking business. He operated the Doherty Funeral Home after his father's retirement, out of this house, until 1969. That year he merged with the Stephenson Funeral Home across the street and became the Stephenson Doherty Funeral Home. In the absence of the funeral home, the building was leased to the Drapery Boutique business in 1969. They operated out of this house until 1970 when the First Savings and Loan Association of Saginaw purchased the building from Michael Doherty. The house was torn down in 1971 for the construction of the new First Savings and Loan Association bank building.

Photograph from the Forrest Meek Collection

808 North McEwan Street
1888 to 1973

Alfred J. Doherty could arguably be considered the most successful citizen to live in Clare. However, that success did not come easily. The early years of Doherty's life in Clare were a struggle. Until he started his hardware business in 1885, he had to be content with working a number of ordinary jobs. As a result, it took him some time before he was in a place of financial stability. When he constructed his first house in 1883, he needed to borrow $50.00 to cover the down payment for the lot. While working as a teacher he also sold insurance in order to supplement his income. It is also told that while teaching at the Dover school, Doherty walked to and from the school. This is most likely because he could not afford to purchase a proper means of transportation.

Doherty also started out small when it came to his political career. The first political office he held started in 1879 when he was elected to the office of city assessor. He distinguished himself so well in that position that in 1885 he was elected as the city clerk. He once again advanced his political career by being elected to the state senate in 1901, 1903 and 1905. Finally, he was also elected to one term as Clare's mayor starting in 1920.

The rise of A. J. Doherty was summarized in the following article from the July 5, 1895, issue of the *Clare Sentinel and Democrat-Press*;

A. J. Doherty
The Man Who Helped Make Clare What She Is Today

Citizens of Clare need look no further than their own city to find a most striking example of what good, honest enterprise and indefatigable energy will accomplish when directed in the right channels. We have that example in the person of A. J. Doherty. Though still a young man, Mr. Doherty has seen nearly all sides of life. He began like many another at the very bottom of the ladder and by his own efforts has climbed to the vicinity of the top rung.

He first came to the city from New York in 1877 and found employment in a mill here as a fireman. In 1880 he taught school for a while, and the people recognizing his ability and integrity elected him school commissioner, which office he held for six years. From then on his rise was meteoric…

To give a complete review of Mr. Doherty's career in Clare would be to write the history of the city from the time he came here. He has been so closely identified with its enterprise that to write of one would be to sketch the other. That he is extremely popular among the citizens goes without saying, and it is difficult to imagine how it could be otherwise.

Another example of the good will felt between Doherty and the City of Clare occurred in 1905. Doherty, as head of both the city electric light plant and water works, and with ten years left on his contract, proposed the sale of both to the City of Clare. Doherty was looking toward the future when the citizens would demand public ownership of both utilities. He offered to sell both at a designated price, but if that price could not be agreed upon he would accept the price to be determined by a third party. The decision of the City of Clare was to have Doherty continue to operate both utilities for the present and into the near future. In the end, Doherty not only continued to own the utilities, but also to upgrade them, and in the case of the water works, constructed a new facility in 1906 near the city park. Doherty was in charge of the light and power company until 1911, when he sold to the Detroit based Consolidated Light and Power Company.

Doherty constructed this house in 1888. At the time he was living in a house on State Street and used this house as a rental property. He sold the property to Elizabeth Michael in 1920. She sold it the following year to Thomas and Alice Groves.

Thomas Groves was born in 1876 in Paulding County, Ohio. He married Alice Burkett, also of Paulding County, in 1899. After their marriage, they moved to Chicago, and in 1907 purchased a farm in Greenwood Township, Clare County. They eventually moved to the City of Clare, and in 1915 purchased the Valley Restaurant at 120 West Fourth Street in Clare. Thomas owned the restaurant for a few years but eventually sold it and went into the automobile and insurance business. A review of the historic newspapers found no mention of Thomas Groves in either of those lines of work. He was most known for being an auctioneer, which he worked at on the side from 1915 until his death. In 1931 he petitioned the city to locate two gas pumps on his property along McEwan Street. The city granted his request and he worked at his gas station from then on. Thomas Groves passed away in 1942. His wife Alice lived here until she sold the house to Bertram and Betty Schleicher in 1956.

The Schleichers came to Clare in 1956 from Birmingham, Michigan. Bertram was originally from Saginaw where he worked in the grocery business. He attended school in Birmingham and later worked as a finish carpenter, and then as a sales representative for a tool manufacturer. Bertram engaged in the real estate business while living in Clare. The Schleichers used a portion of their house as a rental apartment. The newspapers list a few newlywed couples who rented here in 1959 and the early 1960s. The known couples who rented here were, Jay and Arlene Poet (1959), John and Gayla Seiter (1962) and Leonard and Lois McJames (1963). Bertram passed away sometime after 1962, and Betty sold the house to Roy and Barbara Dunbar in 1968.

Roy Dunbar was born in 1927 and originated from Flint. He served in World War II and re-enlisted for one year in 1945. After his discharge, he moved to Lake Station. He married Barbara Jean Zinser, who was from Clare, in 1948. Starting in 1950 Roy began working in the real estate business, a profession he worked in until his death. The Dunbars moved to Clare in 1954. Roy passed away while living in this house in 1970. Barbara continued to own the house and rent it to the Clare Real Estate Mart until 1973.

The final owner of this house was the First Savings and Loan Association of Saginaw. They had previously purchased the house at 806 North McEwan in 1970 and tore it down the next year to make room for their new bank building. The First Savings and Loan Association purchased this house in 1973 in order to tear it down for the construction of a parking lot on the north side of their bank.

Photograph from the Forrest Meek Collection

821 North McEwan Street
1889 to 1961

This house has historically been known as the Lew and Nellie Davy house. Except for the first year and a half of their marriage, they lived here the whole time they were together. But Lew and Nellie were not the first owners of this house. That honor goes to Dr. Francis and Minnie Todd.

Dr. Francis Todd came to Clare around 1882. He was educated at the University of Michigan and eventually had his office on the second floor of the Clare County Bank building. He married Minnie Beebe in 1886, and had this house built three years later. Dr. and Mrs. Todd left Clare and moved to Oakland, California, in either 1893 or 1894. The Davys purchased the house in spring of 1894.

Lew Davy was born in Warren, Michigan in 1869. His obituary states that he "started to fend for himself at the age of

Lew Davy
Photograph from the
Clare Sentinel 1904

Lew Davy
Photograph from the
Clare Sentinel 1963

thirteen, under the watchful eye of his older brother V. R. Davy."
His brother Vernal owned a dry goods store in Evart. Lew came to
Clare in 1893 to establish the Davy Department Store here. The store
was first located in the Wolskey block. In 1895 Lew Davy along
with Robert Mussell and William Elden constructed a three-store
brick building, with the Davy store in the south unit. Davy
purchased the Rockafellow wood frame store building adjacent to
his brick building at the northwest corner of Fourth and North
McEwan Streets in 1900. Four years later he constructed a new brick
building on the same corner of Fourth and North McEwan Streets.
Davy tore down his wood frame building and used the site for the
south half of his new building, and at the same time used his existing
brick building for the north half.

Lew and Vernal worked closely together in the Davy store
business, with Lew in Clare, and Vernal in Evart. Vernal owned an
interest in the Clare store until he sold it to Lew in 1925.

159

Nellie Stout was born in 1868 and was from the Cedar Springs, Michigan area. Lew and Nellie were married in 1892 in Evart, and they moved to Clare the following year. Nellie was just as much a part of the Davy store as Lew, working there until 1953.

In addition to owning the Davy Store, Lew also served as the Clare Postmaster for the four years of the Herbert Hoover administration. He was also named the Clare "citizen of the year" in 1957. Lew also had the honor of owning one of the first automobiles in Clare, and he continued to drive until he was ninety-three years old.

After being ill for a period of three years Nellie Davy passed away in 1955, and Lew passed away in 1963. After his death, the Davy store was sold to Glen C. Folkert, who converted it to one of his Mill End Stores. This house was torn down in 1965. The property was purchased by the Citizens State Bank, which constructed their building immediately to the south of Davy's house in 1961.

821 North McEwan Street
Unknown date, looking Southwest
Photograph from the Forrest Meek Collection

Photograph from the Forrest Meek Collection

406 East Sixth Street
1893 to 2001

Charles Smalley constructed this house in 1893. Two years after the house was built Mr. Smalley petitioned the city to build a bridge on Sixth Street that would span the Little Tobacco Drain near his home. The city denied his request, and as a result, the bridge was not constructed until 1903.

The Smalley's moved to Pinconning in 1898, but did not sell the house until 1903. They sold to Frank and Maude Blain. Frank was responsible for building the addition onto the house that served as the kitchen and wood-house. The only information that could be found on Frank Blain was that he worked as the local representative for the E. G. Dailey Company of Detroit. An advertisement from 1907 stated he was looking for farmers to grow cucumbers to be processed at the salting station at Clare. The Blains lived in this house until 1916 when they moved to California.

The house was sold at that time to Herbert and Nellie Allen. Herbert was born in 1848 in Lockporte, New York. He graduated in 1876 from the Syracuse School of Law. He worked as a lawyer for four years, but failing health forced him to seek work that would take him outdoors. In 1880 he settled on a farm in Gilmore Township, Isabella County. Two years later he married Mary Dunnigan. Herbert and Mary moved to Clare in 1891, but after nineteen years of marriage Mary passed away. Hebert married Nellie Graham sometime after 1901, and they lived in this house from 1916 until they sold it to Clarence and Carrie Mance in 1919.

The Mances owned the house until 1921 when they sold it to George and Ada Easler. George Easler was known for his furniture business which was located on the 100 Block of East Fourth Street in downtown Clare. He retired from active business the same year he purchased this house. It is unlikely that they lived in this house, but used it for a rental property. About the same time, they purchased this house they also purchased other rental houses in Clare. The Easler's residence was on the 100 Block of West Sixth Street. The Easler's sold this house to Charles and Kate Knapp in 1928, after the Knapp home on the north end of Cedar Street in Clare was destroyed by fire.

Ada and George Easler
Photograph from the
Forrest Meek Collection

Charles Knapp, whom his friends always called Lyle from his middle name, Carlisle, was born in 1896 in St. Croix Falls, Wisconsin. When he was six months old he moved with his parents and located in Chesaning, Michigan. He later came to Clare County with his family and settled in Sheridan Township. He married Kate Bell in 1913, who was also from Sheridan Township, and they took up residence on the Knapp family farm.

Kate and Lyle Knapp
Photograph from the
Robert Knapp Collection

Lyle moved his family to the city of Clare in 1918 and entered into the real estate business. In 1919 he took the family west, to Washington State, intending to emigrate. But his wife, Kate, objected to the move and the family returned in 1920. He was employed in 1920 with the E. A. Strout Farm Agency selling farm land in the Clare area. He sold his farm in Sheridan Township in 1922, and the following year moved to Flint where he worked for the Buick Motor Company. During his time in Flint, he continued to own this home but advertised it for rent. By 1940 Lyle Knapp was back in Clare and opened his own C. C. Knapp Realty Agency, which he operated out of this house. He suffered a stroke in 1947 that left him without speech, and he passed away in 1957. His wife Kate lived in a portion of this house until her death in 1974, while the remainder of the house served as rentals. The entire house was a rental property after Kate's passing.

In 1975 the house was purchased by Julius and Kathleen Mihalyfi. Julius passed away in 1978 and Kathleen sold the house to Robert and Loretta Mihalyfi in 1980. After their divorce, the house was deeded to Robert Mihalyfi in 1985. Robert sold the house to Timmy and Linda Blain in 1987, and Timmy sold it to Lloyd Donald in 2000. A house fire in 2001 damaged the house's second story. It was deemed unrepairable and was torn down.

Photograph from Clare Remembered

601 East Sixth Street
1902 to 2000

Edwin Stearns was born in 1844 in Pittsfield Massachusetts. He moved to Jackson, Michigan, when he was a youth. In 1861, at the age of seventeen, he enlisted in Company F, 20th Regiment, Michigan Infantry. He served the entire duration of the Civil War despite being wounded in combat twice.

Edwin married Mary Hinman in 1869. Mary was from Jeddo, New York, born in 1843, and was one of thirteen children. Mary came to Michigan in 1866. They came to Vernon Township in 1880 and from then on lived the life of a farmer. In 1902, at the age of fifty-eight, he built this house on the five-acre lot known as the old Fick farm.

The following year John White's brother-in-law William Becker purchased this house and five-acre property for John in anticipation of his move to Clare. John White was born in Armagh, Ireland, in 1859. He graduated from the Armagh University with a

164

degree in civil engineering and later continued his education in England. His father was also a civil engineer. He came to the United States at the age of twenty-two and began work as a bridge engineer for the Pennsylvania Railroad System.

When the Ann Arbor Railroad was being constructed through Clare in 1887, John met his future wife, Anna Becker. Anna came to Clare with her family in 1881 and married John White in 1888. After the completion of the Ann Arbor Railroad in 1893, John moved his family to Owosso and worked as the Chief Engineer of the railroad. They resided in Owosso for ten years and then moved to Toledo where he served as the Chief Engineer for the Wheeling Lake Erie Railroad. John brought his family to Clare in 1903 and settled in this house.

In his obituary found in the November 26, 1943, issue of the *Clare Sentinel*, the paper chronicled his engineering career as follows:

> Mr. White was a pioneer railroad and highway builder. He was Chief Engineer of Surveys and Superintendent of Construction of the Ann Arbor Railroad, The Baltimore and Washington Electric, The Middle Tennessee Railroad, Middle Tennessee Electric Railroad, Toledo and Bryan Electric, The Toledo, Monroe and Detroit and Toledo and Western.
>
> Mr. White also held the position of City Engineer of Bowling Green, Wauseon, Ohio, and Alma, Michigan.
>
> From 1918 to 1923 he was Project Engineer for the Michigan State Highway Department, which position he resigned when elected County Engineer in Clare County.
>
> In 1932 he retired from Engineering and entered a partnership with his son Edward, in the firm of Whites Greenhouse and Nursery, of Clare, a work he loved and enjoyed until he was stricken with

arthritis three years ago and confined to bed for the last seven months..."

Anna White lived in this house until her death in 1932, and her husband John followed her in 1943. The house was inherited by John and Anna's son Edward and his wife Viola, but they had been living here since shortly after their marriage.

Edward was born in 1890, and when he was very young the family moved to Owosso, then to Toledo and finally to Clare in 1903. He studied horticulture at the Michigan Agricultural College in 1913. Edward married Viola Hawley in 1928. Viola was born in 1897 and was a native of Ludington, Michigan. The couple moved to Clare after their marriage, and Edward started his nursery business on the property surrounding this

Edward B. White
Photograph from the
Clare Sentinel 1960

house in 1929. The September 29, 1933, issue of the *Clare Sentinel* recounts an almost tragic event that occurred in this house during a lightning storm.

Mr. and Mrs. Edward A. White of the Whites' Fruit and Floral Farm, at the east end of 6th street, miraculously escaped serious injury about three o'clock Monday morning when lightning entered their home during the severe electric storm that passed over this section of the state.

166

Mr. and Mrs. White and the two smaller children occupied a bedroom at the southeast corner of the house, while another slept just outside the door. The bolt of lightning struck a large elm tree just outside the room. Glancing from the tree it entered the building and passed along in a horizontal line four feet above their fifteen-month-old baby, in its bed. Here it exploded and divided, one bolt going to the ground, while the other jumped to the eavestrough and followed it around the south side of the house to the ground, burning off both the telephone and electric wires.

In the dark Mr. and Mrs. White tried to find the two children, but the plaster and splinters which had been thrown broadcast over the room made the task difficult. The second oldest child had luckily slid down under the quilts while sleeping and a thick piece of plaster twelve inches square was found on the pillow. The smallest child had to be dug out of a pile of plaster which covered the bed. None of the four occupants of the room were injured in any way.

As soon as possible both Edward and his father John White made a search of the house, but no fire had been set.

The house suffered considerable damage. The window casing was torn out, sheeting and siding torn to splinters and plaster was thrown across the room with such force as to knock the paint and varnish from the woodwork.

Edward lived in the house and operated White's Fruit and Floral Farm until the 1930s. It was then changed to White's Greenhouse and Nursery and in 1966 to White's Nursery and Garden Center. Edward White passed away in 1967; his wife Viola continued to live here until her death in 1983.

Edward and Viola's son Ed White acquired the house after the death of Viola. The house was razed by the Clare Fire

Department in 2000. The house needed to be removed for the creation of the Woods Nursery Subdivision. The burning of the house was an educational opportunity for the Clare Fire Department.

Photograph from the Forrest Meek Collection

113 East Fifth
1904 to 1988

Frank Doherty built this house 1904. It was constructed of pressed brick from the Sebewaing Sandstone Brick Company. The company was so proud of the construction of the house that they made it a model home for their brick products.

Frank Doherty was born to Alfred and Alice Doherty in 1880. He attended Clare Schools and studied at Olivet College. In 1897 he joined his father and brother Floyd in the A. J. Doherty & Sons hardware business. His father's election to the state senate resulted in A. J. Doherty retiring from the hardware business and turning it over to his two sons in 1903. The following year Floyd sold his interest in the business to Frank. By the end of the decade, Frank himself was out of the hardware business and was acting as superintendent of the local electric light plant. The power plant

Frank Doherty
Photograph from the
Clare Sentinel 1903

changed ownership to the Consolidated Light and Power Company out of Detroit in 1911 and retained Doherty in his position as superintendent.

Frank Doherty continued with the Consolidated Light and Power Company and was transferred to Mackinac Island in 1917 to run the electrical plant there. At that time James Stewart and Alberta Bicknell became owners of this house.

James was born in Saginaw, in 1874, to Nathan and Martha Bicknell. When the Bicknells moved to Clare, James was only six weeks old. He graduated from the Clare schools and also received a Pharmaceutical Degree from the Detroit College of Medicine.

For four-and-a-half years, starting in 1896, he lived in Shepherd and operated a department store. James returned to Clare in 1900, working with his father in the general merchandise business. In 1911, James left the retail business and accepted a position as Director and Cashier of the Citizens State Bank. He was elected as bank president in 1927 and held that position until his death. While working at the bank James Bicknell had an excellent reputation around the state and was elected President of the Group Five Michigan Bankers Association in 1937. He also served as president of the Clare Chamber of Commerce and as a member of the Clare School Board. During the construction of the new school in the 1920s, Bicknell was the School Board Treasurer.

James married Alberta Long from Richmond, Michigan, in 1897. Alberta was the daughter of a Congregational Church minister from Paris, Illinois and was born in 1877. James passed away in 1943, Alberta did not see death until 1983, living to the age of 105.

A. J. Doherty III purchased the house after the death of Alberta Bicknell. He first leased the building to Sheridan Realty for their real estate office. By the latter part of the 1980s, Reiss Real Estate was leasing it for the same purpose. The house was torn down in the fall of 1988 for the eastward expansion of the Doherty Hotel.

James Stewart Bicknell
Photograph from the
Forrest Meek Collection

Photograph from the Forrest Meek Collection

813 North McEwan Street
1904 to 1961

Frederick Lister was born in Cambridge, England, in 1854. His father died when Frederick was nine years old, and ten years later he came to the United States. He first settled in Buffalo, New York, where he married his first wife Margaret. They moved to Clare County in 1876, where he started farming. Margaret passed away in 1881, and Frederick moved into the Village of Clare in about 1892. After his farming days, Mr. Lister embarked on a career in the lumber business. He first partnered with George S. Archbold, and then with Henry Ort. The Ort partnership ended in 1896.

Frederick Lister married Anna Belle Stevens in 1895. She was born in Eaton County, Michigan in 1873, and moved to Clare with her parents, Henry and Mary Stevens, in 1880. Fred and Anna purchased the house at 206 West Seventh Street in 1897 but were renting it prior to that. In 1900 Frederick and Anne moved to Millersburg in Presque Isle County, Michigan, where he purchased a large parcel of timber land. For the next four years, he harvested and milled the lumber from his land.

Lister returned to Clare in 1903, and along with George Benner, J. R. Goodman, and C. H. O'Donald, was instrumental in organizing the Citizens Bank in Clare. He had this house on McEwan Street constructed in 1904. Besides his interest in banking Lister also continued his work in the lumber industry.

He continued working until his death due to stomach cancer in 1908. After Frederick's death, Anna began renting out rooms in her house. The first advertisement seen in the newspaper for this is in 1917, but she was renting to James Bicknell as early as 1914. In the 1920s she opened The

Fred Lister
Photograph from
A History of Northern
Michigan and its People
by Perry Powers

Adore Beauty Shop in her house. Anna Belle Lister continued to live in this house until she moved to Ann Arbor in 1926. She continued to own the house until the mid-1930s and rented it out. One of Clare's oil men, Mr. R. Roan, and his wife, were renting the house in 1932.

Bert Kane purchased the house in 1935. Bert Kane originated from Mount Pleasant and was born in 1897. He served in World War I and then moved to Saginaw. Bert married Fredrika Lockwood in 1924.

Fredrika was a native of Harrison, born in 1900, and went on to graduate from the Central State Teachers College. She taught in the rural schools of Clare County, and finished her teaching career in the primary grades of Fancher School in Mount Pleasant. After their marriage, they resided in Harrison where Bert owned the Ohio Tavern (later known as the Surrey House). Fredrika passed away in 1931 while they were living in Harrison. Bert Kane sold the Ohio Tavern to Mr. and Mrs. Ray J. Kear in 1935, and moved to this house in Clare the same year.

While in Clare, Bert Kane was named the sales manager for the Wurlitzer Music Manufacturing Co. He was in charge of sales, distribution, and service for the area north of Lansing including the Upper Peninsula. By 1943 Bert Kane had moved to Detroit, and he sold this house to Floyd and Clara Luke in 1944.

Floyd Luke was born in 1894 in Lenawee County, Michigan. Floyd spent his childhood farming in Lenawee County, then moved with his parents to Fulton County, Ohio, and finally to Monroe County, Michigan. He married Clara Flaishans in 1917.

Clara was born in 1896 in Wyandotte and moved with her parents to the "Headquarters Farm" in Frost Township, Clare County in 1908. In 1914 she moved to Flat Rock, Michigan, where she met Floyd Luke. The couple lived in Flat Rock and operated a trucking business until they moved to Clare in 1944.

Floyd was the manager of the Sinclair Service Station located on the corner of McEwan and State Streets. He also converted this house into what was known as the "Luke Tourist Home." Floyd passed away in 1955 while still owning this house. His wife Clara sold the house to Frank and Helen Holbrook two months after his death. Mr. and Mrs. Russell Allan took over the operation of the tourist home and changed the name to the "Allan Tourist Home."

It was the Allans' intention to purchase the house and continue to operate their tourist home. However, the Citizens State Bank purchased the house in 1960 and dismantled it the next year to make room for its new bank building.

Photograph from the Forrest Meek Collection

717 North McEwan Street
1915 to 1976

This is the fifth house that Alfred and Alice Doherty called their residence and the one they spent their final days in. The house was located on a lot on the southwest corner of McEwan and Seventh Streets. Doherty purchased the lot in 1913 from Mrs. Henrietta Derby. The lot contained a house which Doherty dismantled in 1914. He then used the materials to construct a double house on a lot he purchased on Wheaton Avenue. Doherty finished the construction of this house in 1915.

Doherty continued to stay active in the latter years of his life. He continued to work as a lobbyist for the Pullman Railroad Car Company. He was elected as mayor of Clare and served one term from April 1920 to April 1922.

175

His most famous contribution to the City of Clare came in the early 1920s when he constructed the Doherty Hotel. The Doherty Hotel sits on the former site of the Calkins House hotel.

The Calkins House was constructed in 1891 and burned in 1920. John Calkins, the proprietor of the hotel, was seventy-three years old when the building burned and had no plans to rebuild the hotel. After the lot sat vacant for one year, A. J. Doherty agreed to construct a new hotel there for an amount totaling at least $60,000.00. The hotel took four years to build, he went through two building contractors, and the cost exceeded $200,000.00. Doherty was in charge of the hotel until 1928, when his son Alfred Doherty II became president.

Alfred J. Doherty
Photograph from the
Forrest Meek Collection

The popularity of the Doherty Hotel and the importance it served in the community of Clare can be best summed up from the following excerpt from the Clare Downtown Historic District, National Register of Historic Places Nomination:

The main reason for the popularity of the Doherty Hotel was its location at the intersection of key highways. At the time the Doherty Hotel was constructed, the major roads coming through Clare were State Highway M-14 (McEwan Street), which ran north and south, and State Highway M-20 (Fifth Street), which ran east and west. Both were still dirt roads at the time. The key to drawing automobile traffic from the south to the northern vacation areas was the paving of these two roads. In the mid-1920s there was tremendous competition between communities for state funding to pave roads. In addition, there was talk that M-14 would be rerouted and bypass Clare altogether. In 1925 Clare natives Dennis Alward, A. Ray Canfield, and Alfred J. Doherty began lobbying Washington D. C. to have M-14 designated as a military road between Lansing and Camp Grayling, the state's National Guard training camp, located sixty miles north of Clare, which would make it eligible for federal funding for concrete paving. With the help of Congressman Roy Woodruff, they were successful, but it was not until 1932 that the pavement actually reached Clare. In 1926 M-20 became US-10, and M-14 became US-27 (now US-127), and the Doherty Hotel then stood at the intersection of two major federal highways heading north connecting downstate cities with popular northern recreation destinations. As a result, most tourist traffic from southeast and south-central Michigan traveled through downtown Clare on its way north. In addition, Clare was approximately halfway between Michigan's southeastern cities and northern vacation areas, which made Clare – and the Doherty – popular dining and overnight locations before the remainder of the journey north.

Alfred Doherty passed away in 1929. His wife Alice lived in this house until her death in 1932. At some unknown time after Alice's passing Charles Strange rented the house, and he rented until at least 1938. Strange was an oil man who located here from Texas. He rented this house while at the same time rented office space at the Doherty Hotel.

James McKay
Photograph from the
Clare Sentinel 1946

James and Mary McKay purchased this house in 1943 as their retirement home. James was born in Simco County, Ontario Canada in 1867. At the age of twelve, he came with his parents and settled on a farm in Vernon Township, then moved to Detroit in 1890. While in Detroit, James became a very successful building contractor. He was associated with the Michigan Contracting Company which built the first electric rail lines from Detroit to Mount Clemens, Jackson to Albion, Grand Rapids to Holland, and Dayton to Miamisburg, Ohio. He was also associated with W. E. Currie in the development and transformation of Hog Island into Belle Isle near Detroit. In 1919 he established the James McKay & Sons Contracting Company. The company owned the first power paving machine in the City of Detroit. James and his sons went on to construct cement paved roadways throughout the State of Michigan.

On December 18, 1894, James McKay purchased a farm north of Clare, and the day after that he married Mary Hudson of Dover. Mary was born in 1876 in Clare County. The McKay farm became famous for the discovery of a natural gas field in 1929. James lived in this house until his death in 1946. Mary survived him and owned the house until her death in 1954.

After her passing, the house was owned by Mary's son, J. Donald McKay, and his wife Dorcas. The Citizens State Bank acquired the house in 1956, and the bank sold it to Marvin Witbeck sometime before 1960. Elmer and Helen Anderson purchased the house in 1960 and owned it until 1972. At that time the house was bought by Jack and Alma Tice who owned it until 1976. During the early 1970s, the house was used as an office building. In 1973 Nivison & Associates Accounting & Tax Services was using the building, and from 1974 to 1976 the Mid States Land Company was leasing here. The house was purchased by Dr. E. C. Shurlow in 1976. It was torn down that same year and replaced with a medical clinic.

717 North McEwan Street
Front of House Looking West, Circa 1970
Photograph from the Forrest Meek Collection

Photograph from the Robert Knapp Collection

Kilarney Farm
1897 to ?

Just as we began this book with a house not located in Clare, it seems appropriate to end it with another non-Clare house. This house was located approximately four-and-a-half miles south of Clare. It was constructed by A. J. Doherty in 1897. This was one of his residences until he built his house at the northeast corner of McEwan and Seventh Streets in 1904.

It was not uncommon for businessmen in the City of Clare to also own farms. A look at the county atlases printed around the start of the twentieth century will show the names of many known businessmen who owned acreage in both Vernon and Grant Townships. A. J. Doherty was no exception. But what made Mr. Doherty different was the scale to which he farmed.

Doherty purchased what was known as the Kelley farm from William Callam in 1896. At the time it was considered the largest and one of the best farms in Isabella County. It contained 640 acres (the equivalent of an entire section of land), with nearly all of it

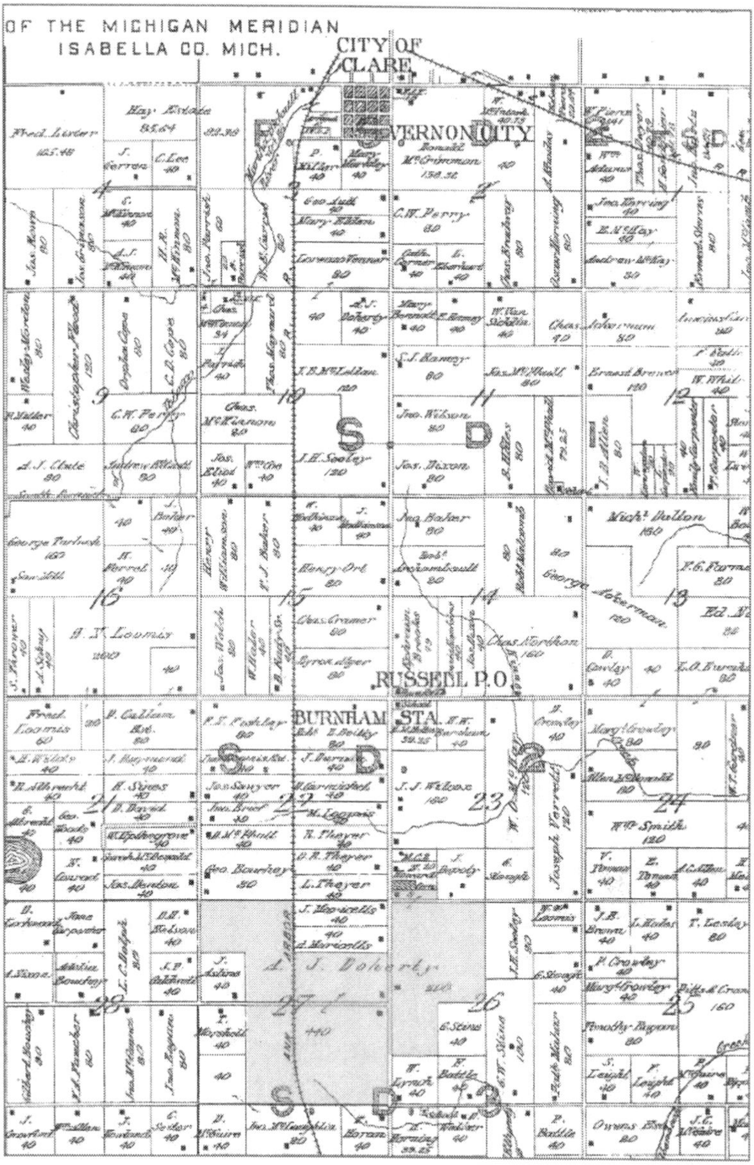

The gray section in the above map shows the area which comprised the Doherty farm in Vernon Township. Doherty also owned a forty acre plot one mile south of Clare, in the northeast quarter of Section 10. This map is taken from the *Plat book of Isabella County, Michigan / drawn from actual surveys and the county records by C. M. Foote & E. C. Hood, 1899.*

181

Alfred and Alice Doherty
Alfred Doherty drawing from the Clare Sentinel 1900
Alice Doherty drawing from the Clare Sentinel 1896

cleared, and as the *Clare Courier* reported on December 4, 1896 "in a high state of cultivation." The farm was devoted primarily to raising livestock, and Doherty referred to it as Kilarney Farm.

In early 1904 Doherty began building a cheese factory on the farm. The idea of locating a factory in Vernon Township instead of the City of Clare put some friction between Doherty and the city fathers. Doherty petitioned the city to reduce the business tax, but their unwillingness resulted in the factory being located on the Kilarney Farm instead of within the City of Clare.

In addition, 1904 saw Doherty's farm being selected as a U. S. government agricultural experiment station. The primary purpose of the station was to study the Hessian fly and how it affected wheat production. This was one of five stations located in Michigan, the others being in Bellaire, Lansing, Hudson and Sault Ste. Marie.

Doherty's interest in owning a farm came to an end in 1911. He originally paid $10,000 for the property but had improved it to such a state that he was able to sell it for $46,000. Charles & Katherine Rexroth, who already owned a 400-acre farm in Bucyrus Ohio, purchased the farm in Vernon Township. Doherty's farm was better equipped with buildings and a nice house, so Rexroth moved here instead of improving his Ohio farm.

Charles Rexroth began to subdivide the farm starting in 1913. The portion of the farm containing this house along with 360 acres, located on the west side of what was to become Mission Road, was sold to Joseph and Ida Page. Page turned around and sold it that same year to a real estate man from Mount Pleasant named Walter Caple. Walter Caple's brother, William Caple, was a real estate

Walter Caple Farm
Photograph from the Forrest Meek Collection

agent in Clare.

A Chicago man named C. V. Abeele acquired the farm in 1917, and Dr. Edward Reiss of Terre Haute, Indiana purchased the farm in 1918. Reiss was the secretary of the Michigan Dairies Company. The company's plan was to modernize the farm with $250,000 of capital and increase dairy production. The farm changed ownership again in 1924 when it was purchased by J. A. Bowman. George House owned the farm starting in 1946 and sold it to a relative in 1957. It is unknown as to when and how this grand home was lost, but it was known to exist during Walter Caple's ownership.

Kilarney Farm
Unknown Date
Photograph from the Forrest Meek Collection

183

Final Word

On January 9, 1938, the men photographed in the picture below gathered to celebrate the seventy-ninth birthday of John White. Of the men pictured here four owned houses that were featured in this book. One other was mentioned as being a business owner in the City of Clare. It is my hope that after reading this book you could look at a photograph like this and not see just a group men. On the other hand I hope you see a group of individuals who contributed to the growth of the City of Clare. They were people who lived here, shared their lives with one another, conducted business together, and were friends. This book is filled with people who had similar experiences, and we only read about fifty houses in Clare. Clare is filled with hundreds of historic houses. Maybe further research will tell the story of the men in this photograph who are not mentioned in this book, and many others that are equally interesting.

Standing from left to right: **Horace Joyner, Dan Vincent, Arthur Bellinger, William Lowery, Simon Bogardus, and John White.** *Seated from left to right:* **John A. Jackson, Thomas Holbrook, William Becker, and Dell Komp.**
Photograph from the Forrest Meek Collection

Bibliography

The houses in this book are listed below and followed by a list of abbreviated sources specific to each building. The abbreviations for the newspaper sources are defined as follows: *CP = Clare Press, CCP = Clare County Press, Cour = Clare Courier, CD = Clare Democrat, CDP = Clare Democrat and Press, CSDP = Clare Sentinel & Democratic Press, Sent = Clare Sentinel, CCC = Clare County Cleaver, ICE = Isabella County Enterprise.* For all buildings, property ownership information was obtained through deeds located at the Clare County Register of Deeds Office, Harrison, Michigan. Tax assessment data at the Clare County Treasurers Office, Harrison, Michigan. In addition, information about businesses and business owners was taken from the *National Register of Historic Places Nomination for the Clare Downtown Historic District.*

Part I Historic Homes

702 Center Avenue, Bay City, Michigan

Gansser, Augustus H. "William McEwan." *History of Bay County, Michigan and Representative Citizens.* Richmond and Arnold, Chicago. 1905. Web. 6 May 2017.

Page, H. R. "William McEwan." *The History of Lake Huron Shore, Michigan, With Illustrations and Biographical Sketches of Some of its Prominent Men and Pioneers.* H. R. Page & Company, Chicago. 1883. Web. 6 May 2017.

"William McEuen," *Michigan Historical Collections.* Michigan Historical Society, 1888. Web. 6 May 2017.

409 Dunlop Street

CCP: 5/7 and 9/17/1881, *Sent*: 7/15/1904, 5/5/1905, 1/15/1909, 12/12/1918, 10/2/1919, 4/19/1946, 7/13/1961, 7/19/1962, 10/17/1963.

301 East Fifth Street

CCP: 8/13/1880, 8/27/1881, *CSDP*: 7/5/1895, *Sent*: 4/23 and 4/30/1943, 2/16/1945, 7/2/1948, 4/29/1949, 10/22/1964, 11/18/1997.

201 East Sixth Street

CCP: 7/13 and 10/19/1883, *CDP*: 2/7 and 4/11/1890, *CSDP*: 7/5/1895, *Sent*: 8/24/1894, 4/30, 5/14 and 12/10/1897, 1/7 and 3/18/1898, 7/28 and 9/8/1899, 5/17 and 10/4/1907, 9/21 and 11/2/1916, 2/22/1917, 2/26/1932, 6/25/1937, 3/17/1939, 9/25/1942, 3/23 and 7/17/1951, 10/7/1970, 5/10/1978, 12/25/1990.

306 East Fifth Street

CCP: 1/30/1880, 7/27/1883, 5/2/1884, *CD*: 5/17/1889, *CDP*: 2/14/1890, *Sent*: 11/20/1902, 7/30/1903, 9/22/1911, 6/29/1923, 9/7/1928, 11/15/1929, 8/15/1941, 8/7/1942, 3/9/1951, 7/12/1962, 9/24/1991.

202 West Seventh Street

CP: 3/28/1884, 9/10/1886, *CD*: 3/15 and 6/7/1889, *CDP*: 8/1/1890, 4/1 and 7/15/1892, 12/13/1895, *Sent*: 10/6/1899, 3/30/1900, 1/3/1913, 3/8/1917, 4/18/1941, 11/12/1943, 10/24/1952, 11/11/1954.

306 West Seventh Street

CCP: 7/24/1885, 1/8/1886, *CDP*: 4/4/1890, *Sent*: 8/25/1893, 9/22 and 10/7/1904, 2/11 and 5/6/1910, 3/16/1928, 5/22/1931, 10/14/1932, 11/16/1934, 7/24/1936, 4/9 and 416/1937, 10/13 and 10/20/1939, 1/19/1940, 6/29/1945, 1/18/1946, 2/6/1948, 2/16/1951, 6/6/1957, 11/19/1964, 6/25/1969.

206 East Fifth Street

CCP: 3/19/1886, *CDP*: 8/7/1891, *CSDP*: 1/11 and 7/5/1895, *Sent*: 8/28/1896, 4/22 and 5/6/1898, 10/31/1901, 5/22/1902, 4/24/1903, 4/ 14 and 7/7/1904, 10/13/1905, 9/13/1907, 7/23 and 7/30 and 11/26/1909, 7/22/1910, 10/6/1911, 8/23 and 10/18/1912, 3/5/1915, 5/15 and 6/19/1925, 11/16/1934, 5/31/1935, 7/18/1941, 10/4 and 11/15/1946, 3/28/1952, 10/2/1953, 8/4/1960, 7/7/1971.

210 West Seventh Street

CCP: 6/1/1883, 9/11/1885, *Sent*: 8/16/1929, 6/3/1949, 2/3/1955.

215 West Seventh Street

CCP: 12/21/1883, *Sent*: 4/24/1902, 1/8/1909, 12/4/1931, 1/24/1947, 3/5/1959, 8/11/1960.

308 East Fifth Street

CCP: 1/15/1886, *CDP*: 2/21 and 12/26/1890, 1/9, 1/16, 4/3 and 8/21/1891 , *ICE*: 10/10/1890, *CSDP*: 3/22/ 1895, 4/17/1896, *Sent*: 10/1/1897, 4/25/1901, 7/30/1903, 5/5/1911, 5/22 and 6/12 and 12/11/1914, 1/8/1915, 11/8/1917, 8/30/1919, 10/21/1921, 11/14/1924, 4/6 and 9/14/1928, 5/30/1930, 1/15 and 10/22/1937, 8/30/1940, 1/21/1948, 12/23/1954

209 West Seventh Street

CP: 5/7/1886, *CSDP*: 6/7/1895, *Sent*: 6/23 and 7/21/1904, 5/17/1907, 1/3/1908, 4/7/1911, 4/4/1913, 4/16/1915, 8/23 and 10/4/1917, 9/23/1921, 1/9/1925, 1/5/1934, 6/14/1935, 8/27/1937, 11/7/1947, 10/25/1956, 1/29/1975.

305 East Fifth Street

CCP: 8/27/21881, *CP*: 10/29/1886, *CDP*: 4/17/1891, *Sent*: 9/7/1894, 5/29/1902, 4/5/1907, 7/6/1928, 3/3 and 8/18/1933, 10/22/1937, 7/21/1939.

301 East State Street

CDP: 1/30 and 11/20/1891, *Sent*: 9/9/1898, 5/19/1899, 7/27/1900, 5/23/1901, 7/30 and 10/1/1903, 8/27/1909, 8/25 and 9/8/1911, 9/26 and 10/17/1913, 8/25/1915, 3/7 and 5/2/1918, 5/12/1921, 3/16/1923, 4/3/1925, 6/21 and 11/8/1940, 2/5/1943, 10/26/1945, 9/3/1964, 3/9/1967, 2/23/1983.

305 West Sixth Street

CCP: 8/21/1885, *CP*: 5/7/1886, *CDP*: 4/24/1891, *CSDP*: 1/4/1895, *Sent*: 5/18, 7/24 and 8/3/1894, 11/2/1900, 2/13/1902, 8/27/1903, 6/19/1908, 6/10/1910,

6/24/1921, 12/19/1924, 2/18/1938, 5/8/1942, 6/8/19452/9 and 11/9/1951, 2/11/1986.

101 Maple Street

Sent: 12/15/1899, 6/20/1901, 8/7 and 10/16/1902, 8/20/1909, 9/16/1910, 10/13 and 12/25/1914, 1/15 and 9/24/1915, 10/24/1924, 12/2/1927, 6/21/1929, 7/13 and 8/10/1945, 11/28/1947, 5/22/1953, 9/3/1954, 1/4/1968.

104 West State Street

CD: 11/13/1891, *Sent*: 6/9/1905, 9/21/1906, 5/16/1913 4/5/1935, 4/16/1937, 12/12/1963.

206 West Seventh Street

CDP: 8/14, 9/18 and 10/16/1891, *CSDP*: 9/20, 10/25 and 11/1/1895, *Cour*: 11/1/1895, *Sent*: 12/2/1892, 4/24/1903, 1/6, 6/16 and 9/29/1905, 5/4/1906, 7/19 and 8/23/1907, 7/8/1910, 1/20/1911, 6/14/1912, 3/12, 9/24, 11/12 and 11/19/1915, 3/25/1922, 11/23/1928, 6/12/1931, 1/24 and 8/14/1936, 10/31/1941, 1/7/1944, 3/5/1948, 10/24/1952, 2/27/1953, 2/8/1962, 5/23/1963, 4/7/1992.

212 West State Street

ICE: 4/7/1875, *CSDP*: 4/26/1895, *Sent*: 10/28/1898, 11/3 and 11/17/1905, 4/6/1906, 9/13/1907, 7/1/1908, 12/23/1923, 11/8/1929, 2/3/1955, 3/5/1959, 7/8/1965.

307 East Fifth Street

CCP: 5/24/1878, *CDP*: 8/15/1890, 3/20/1902, *CSDP*: 11/8/1895, *Sent*: 10/6/1893, 5/28/1897, 10/5/1900, 5/16/1901, 1/7 and 11/4/1910, 11/10/1911, 4/5/1929, 5/31/1935, 8/15/1941, 11/8/1946, 1/30/1948, 1/20/1955, 10/25/1956, 8/28/1990.

310 West Wheaton Avenue

CDP: 7/29/1892, *Sent*: 6/3/1903, 12/23/1923, 5/7/1926, 11/8/1929, 6/1/1934, 7/24 and 11/20/1936, 3/17/1939, 3/7/1941, 12/15/1944, 3/16 and 11/16/1945, 8/20/1948, 4/20/1951, 8/22/1957, 10/22/1959, 11/10/1960.

805 Beech Street

Sent: 9/22/1893, 5/21/1903, 10/27/1905, 4/23/1915, 11/16/1916, 5/28/1937, 3/21/1952, 5/18/1977.

1005 North McEwan Street

CDP: 11/13/1891, *Sent*: 1/8/1897, 2/23/ 1900, 6/13/1901, 11/11/1904, 10/27/1905, 5/8/1908, 7/25/1909, 3/25/1911, 5/14 and 11/5/1915, 10/19/1916, 11/28/1918, 1/19 and 5/25/1923, 2/10/1933, 9/17/1937, 5/17/1946, 8/27 and 12/3/1948, 7/29/1949.

303 East State Street

Cour: 4/17/1896, 7/3//1903, 4/19/1907, *Sent*: 5/5/1893, 5/18 and 11/2/1894, 4/17/1896, 4/22, 8/19 and 12/23/1898, 11/9/1900, 8/21/1902, 7/3/1903, 8/18 and 9/1/1904, 4/19/1907, 10/3/1913, 2/17/1933, 1/21 and 7/1/1938, 8/25/1944, 9/27/1946, 10/12/1951, 1/8/1959.

210 East State Street

CSDP: 1/11/1895, *Sent*: 5/27/1898, 7/6/1900, 4/18/1901, 7/14/1904, 11/24/1911, 7/9/1915, 7/31/1919, 3/18/1920, 4/24 and 7/10/1931, 2/23/1934, 11/29/1940, 9/25/1942, 5/5/1944, 1/31/1947, 11/25/1949, 10/26/1951, 12/25/1953, 11/18/1954, 4/7/1955.

618 North Rainbow Drive

CDP: 2/12/1892, *CSDP*: 1/18 and 3/20/1896, *Sent*: 2/5, 2/19 and 6/5/1903, 11/9 and 11/23/1906, 3/26 and 7/9/1909, 5/3/1912, 2/9/1923, 1/22/1926, 1/12/1940, 2/14/1941, 9/8/1944, 8/6/1948, 8/29/1952, 5/19/1960.

106 West Wheaton Avenue

CSDP: 5/24/1895, *CCC*: 6/3/1938, *Sent*: 5/18/1900, 1/29, 5/14 and 7/3/1903, 6/9/1905, 5/16 and 12/19/1913, 5/27/1932, 7/1/1938, 8/20/ and 9/3/1943, 1/28/1944, 6/11/1948, 7/14/1950, 4/12/1956, 10/6/1982.

314 East Second Street

CSDP: 5/31 and 7/5/1895, *Sent*: 10/4/1907, 3/27 and 11/20/1908, 7/9/1909, 4/15 and 11/11/1920, 3/10 and 9/30/1921, 8/8/1941, 7/19/1962.

203 East Fifth Street

Sent: 3/20/1903, 6/10/1927, 12/27/1912, 5/22/1914, 9/25/1919, 12/9/1920, 9/28/1923, 1/18/1924, 12/16/1925, 1/7 and 7/8/1927, 11/9/1928, 6/7/1929, 5/10 and 10/11/1935, 9/4 and 11/6/1936, 6/25/1937, 10/28/1938, 7/21/1939, 10/18/1940, 8/28 and 9/4/1942, 4/6/1945, 5/30/1952, 11/29/1956, 11/6/1958, 11/6/1975, 2/10/1998.

307 East Sixth Street

CCP: 7/11/1884, *CSDP*: 7/19/1895, *Sent*: 8/27/1903, 4/28 and 8/25/1904, 7/28/1911, 5/30/1913, 3/7/1947, 11/5/1948, 1/17/1957.

313 East Seventh Street

Sent: 7/28/1904, 11/2/1916, 3/10/1921, 12/14/1923, 12/13/1929. 3/20/1936, 8/26/1938, 8/16/1940, 2/15/1946, 10/16/1953, 9/18/1958.

604 Pine Street

Sent: 5/15/1902, 12/17/1903, 12/2/1904, 5/12/1905, 6/22/1906, 3/11/1910, 8/1/1913, 2/3/1922, 1/10/1941, 12/24/1964.

804 North McEwan Street

Sent: 8/25/1904, 6/3/1910, 9/27/1929, 7/12/1946, 12/29/1966.

114 East State Street

CDP: 3/21/1890, 4/24, 7/19 and 9/4/1891, *Sent*: 7/11/1901, 4/21/1905, 4/6, 7/6 and 8/3/1906, 5/14/1909, 5/9 and 9/12/1918, 9/23/1921, 4/27/ and 7/22/1923, 5/14/1930, 11/6/1931, 10/22 and 10/29/1937, 5/10/1940, 4/5 and 8/30/1946, 8/26/1949, 12/29/1950, 5/2/1952, 8/28/1953.

214 East State Street

CDP: 4/3/1891, *Sent*: 8/10/1916, 1/30/1919, 12/1/1922, 4/25/1924, 11/14/1940, 8/2/1946, 6/15/1923, 5/1/1936, 8/27/1937, 11/15/1940, 10/29/1943, 8/31 and 9/21/1945, 11/24 and 12/22/1950, 6/6/1963, 5/13/1981, 9/20/1988.

216 East Seventh Street

Sent: 5/17/1917, 6/12/1919, 9/15/1922, 8/22 and 10/10/1924, 8/16/1935, 6/27/1940.

304 East Sixth Street

Sent: 1/28,1910, 1/26 and 4/17/1914, 4/20/1916, 5/15/1919, 7/3 and 8/5/1920, 4/4/1924, 7/7/1944, 1/19/1945, 2/22/1968, 11/5/1969.

701 Beech Street

Sent: 2/13/1914, 8/7/1919, 8/12/1921, 11/23/1934, 3/1/1935, 1/20/1939, 7/28/1950, 1/31/1963, 1/19 and 8/24/1967, 2/11/1976.

211 East Sixth Street

Sent: 8/10/1916, 4/15/1922, 4/5/1929, 11/20 and 11/27/1942, 8/31/1945, 8/1/1979, *ICE*: 9/5/1919, *Cour*: 3/17/1922.

1601 North McEwan Street

Sent: 4/25/1924, 12/5/1930, 5/20 and 7/17/1932, 5/20/1938, 9/6/1940, 12/17/1964.

Knapp, Robert. *Mystery Man*. Clare, Michigan: Cliophile Press, 2014. Print.

501 East Sixth

Mount Pleasant Times: 6/10/1926, *Sent*: 7/3 and 10/9/1936, 8/8/1941, 12/28/1961, 11/25/1965, 7/24/1981, 11/9/1983, *Gladwin County Record*: 3/28/1979.

Knapp, Robert. *Mystery Man*. Clare, Michigan: Cliophile Press, 2014. Print

208 & 210 East Seventh Street

CD: 4/15/1887, *Sent*: 12/14/1928, 6/28/1935, 5/27 and 10/7/1938, 7/7/1940.

Part II Lost but not Forgotten

107 East Seventh Street

CCP: 8/23/1878, 7/11, 7/18, and 10/24/1884, 5/8/1885, *Sent*: 10/2/1953, 1/22/1954.

111 West Fifth Street

CCP: 3/12 and 12/24/1880, 4/16/1881, 8/8/1884, 8/21/885, *CDP*: 2/7/1890, *Sent*: 8/10/1894, 12/23/1898, 4/12/1912, 11/4/1920, 4/27/1928, 10/7/1938.

806 North McEwan Street

CCP: 8/9/1878, 12/12/1879, 9/10/1880, 5/28 and 7/23/1881, 5/4 and 8/10/1883, 7/11/1884, 12/4/1885, 1/15/1886, *CP*: 10/1/1886, *CDP*: 3/28/1890, 1/2/1891, *CSDP*: 3/1, 6/28 and 7/5/1895, 7/3/1896, *Sent*: 11/17/1893, 5/28/1897, 3/25, 5/6 and 8/19/1898, 6/1 and 7/27 and 12/7/1900, 7/3/1902, 6/18 and 7/16/1903, 7/28 and 12/30/1904, 4/7/1905, 12/14/1906, 5/3/1907, 5/29 and 10/2/1925, 4/29/1927, 9/27/1929, 9/4/1931, 9/8/1933, 5/18 and 6/1/1934, 8/8/1952, 12/8/1966, 4/2 and 5/21/1969, 1/6/1971, 3/2/1977.

808 North McEwan Street

CCP: 6/20/1879, 3/13/1885, *CSDP*: 7/5/1895, *Sent*: 3/22/1917, 4/22/1920, 4/3/1942, 3/5, 12/3 and 1231/1959, 2/8/1962, 8/22/1963, 12/2/1970, 2/10/1971.

821 North McEwan Street

CDP: 1/9/1891, *Sent*: 12/30/1892, 3/23 and 4/20/1894, 9/11/1896, 5/7/1897, 8/11/1955, 5/9/1963, 1/21/1965.

406 East Sixth Street

CSDP; 4/19 and 5/10/1895, *Sent*: 3/11/1898, 6/16/1901, 8/6/1903, 10/28/1904, 3/1/1907, 5/7/1911, 2/13/1919, 11/16/1923, 5/11 and 6/8/1928, 12/18/1831, 12/23/1932, 3/8/1940, 12/18/1942, 10/24/1947, 7/18/1957, 1/1/1975, 9/27/1978.

601 East Sixth Street

Sent: 6/5/1902, 3/26.1903, 9/9/1921, 2/17/1922, 10/14/1932, 9/29/1933, 11/26/1943, 1/26/1967, 6/22/1983.

Lingaur, Kenneth L. "Interview with Edward White Concerning Former House at 601 East Sixth Street, Clare, Michigan". 8 Sept. 2017.

113 East Fifth Street

Sent: 5/13/1898, 3/26 and 7/16/1903, 7/7/1905, 1/21/1910, 1/6 and 11/17/1911, 7/19/1917, 10/31/1930, 3/3/1939, 5/7/1943, 1/12/1983 and 12/13/1988.

813 North McEwan Street

Cour: 6/11/1881, *Sent*: 4/7/1904, 10/30/1908, 10/2/1914, 9/13/1917, 12/7/1923, 8/13/1926, 9/20/1929, 7/24/1931, 7/15/1932, 5/10/1935, 4/24/1936, 7/9/1943, 5/5/1944, 2/10, 4/7 and 7/7/1955, 2/23/1956, 3/12 and 5/21/1959, 1/5/1961, 10/13/1976, 2/11/1997.

Powers, Perry F., and H. G. Cutler. *A History of Northern Michigan and its People.* Chicago: Lewis Pub., 1912. Print.

717 North McEwan Street

Sent: 10/10/1913, 5/8/1914, 7/9/1915, 4/22/1920, 3/17/1922, 11/25/1932, 10/7/1938, 9/27/1946, 12/9/1954, 1/3/1973, 10/23/1974, 7/21/1976.

Kilarney Farm, Vernon Township

Cour; 12/4/1896, *ICE*: 1/1/1897, 3/31/1911, 11/30/1917, 4/12/1918 8/6/1920, *Sent*: 2/12/1897, 3/17 and 8//25/1904, 3/31/1911, 4/25/1913, 10/18/1917.

All photographs except where noted are attributed to the author.

Index of Names

Nolan, Mr. & Mrs. Delbert, 91
Nolan, Delbert Jr., 91

O'Connor, Mr. & Mrs., 95
O'Donald, C. H., 82, 86, 173
O'Meila, Bridget see Bridget
    Jackson
Olson, James & Anna, 128-129,
    136
Olson, George, 129
Olson, Gloria, 129
Ort, Henry, 172
Orth, Sara see Sara Greer
Owens, Elsie see Elsie Brasington

Page, Joseph & Ida, 183
Parrott, Della see Della Heiser
Patton, Earl, 88
Paxton, Richard & Kathleen, 102
Peasley, Kenneth & Opal, 53
Perron, Geneva, see Geneva Edick
Perry, Charles W., 18, 32
Peters, Nelson, 31
Peters, Pearl see Pearl Sanford
Pettit, Charles E., 132
Pettit, Walter & Alta, 132-134
Phinisey, E. R., 50
Phinnesy, John, 147
Pickle, Charles L., 110
Pierce, H. W., 55
Pierson, Ella, 39
Pierson, Jennie, 39
Pierson, Robert & Mary, 39
Plank, Lydia see Lydia Randall
Poet, Jay & Arlene, 157
Poet, Virginia, 84
Porterfield, Maude see Maude
    Callihan
Poulson, Orville, 55
Pratt, Edward & Melissa, 28-30
Presley, Annie, 45
Presley, Thomas, 29, 45

Randall, Albert & Minnie, 54
Randall, Herbert & Lovange, 35-36
Randall, Lydia, 54
Rapson, R. A., 151
Raven, George, 24
Razek, Henry, 68
Reiss, Dr. Edward, 183
Rexroth, Charles, 182-183
Rexroth, Katherine, 182
Riggs, W. D., 86-87
Ritter, Harvey, 74
Roan, Mr. R., 173
Robinson, Ann Jane see Jennie
    Alger
Rockafellow, Rachel see Rachel
    Godman
Roe, Dr. Joseph, 68-69
Roe, Nora, 68
Rogers, Herman, 82
Roof, Mr. & Mrs. William, 58
Rorison, David, 37-38, 89
Rorison, Marie, 37
Rosenstein, Claude, 135
Rosier, Floyd & Beatrice, 36
Rothstein, Arnold, 135
Ross, Giles & Amanda, 76-77
Ross, Velma see Velma Damoth
Ross, William, 76
Roxburgh, Elden & Louise, 53
Roxburgh, Ethel, 53
Rukenbrod, Mr., 151
Ryan, James & Rachel, 136

Sanford, Dr. B. J., 31
Sanford, Dr. Fred C., 30-31, 59, 91
Sanford, Glen, 31
Sanford, Mary, 30-31
Sanford, Pearl, 31
Schleicher, Bertram & Betty, 156-
    157
Schleigel, Irwin & Ethel, 41
Schug, Barbara, 35
Schug, Caroline, 35, 87-88

Wahl, Frank, 99
Wait, Bertelle, 23
Walker, Don, 63
Waller, Edward, 67-68
Waller, Lousie, 67
Walworth, Marjorie, 23
Webb, John, 37
Webb, William, 120
Weeks, Louise see Louise Waller
Weidner, Charles & Olive, 117
Weisman, Louis, 18
Welch, Edgar, 116
Welch, J. L., 37
Wells, Bernice, 33
Wells, George, 33-34
Westmiller, Idella see Idella
    Maynard
White, Anna, 165-166
White, Edward A., 44, 51, 116
White, Edward B., 166-167
White, Edward Jr., 167
White, Jennie, 44
White, John, 164-166, 184
White, Viola, 166-167
Wilkinson, Mr., 95
Willis, D., 82
Wilson, Mrs. J. H., 23
Wilson, John, 94
Wilson, Woodrow, 41
Wise, Esther, 152
Witbeck, Marvin, 74-75
Witbeck, Rolland, 75
Wolskey, William, 18
Wood, Dave, 79
Woodruff, Roy, 177
Woodward, W. J., 41
Worden, Joseph & Lillie, 38
Wright, Ammi, 28, 42
Wylie, Alexander, 47
Wyman, Jay & Mary, 49-50
Wyman, Luman, 50

Zimmerman, Minnie see Minnie
    Edick
Zinser, Barbara Jean see Barbara
    Dunbar

About the Author

Ken Lingaur is a native of Lake Leelanau, Michigan, and has lived in Clare since 2003. He earned his Master's Degree in Historic Preservation from Eastern Michigan University in 2014, and the following year founded Lingaur Preservation LLC.

Lingaur Preservation LLC is a historic preservation consulting firm specializing in the research and documentation of historic places.

Ken Lingaur has been married since 1995, and along with his wife Sherrie have four boys.

For more information on Lingaur Preservation LLC visit the website at www.lingaurpreservation.com.

Made in the USA
Middletown, DE
07 August 2018